* * *

ESSENTIAL

[yard care and landscaping projects]

improving and caring for your yard

[contents]

THIS OLD HOUSE ®
ESSENTIAL YARD CARE AND
LANDSCAPING PROJECTS,
A *THIS OLD HOUSE* ® BOOK
BY THE EDITORS OF
THIS OLD HOUSE MAGAZINE

PRINTED IN THE UNITED
STATES OF AMERICA
NEW YORK, NEW YORK

FIRST EDITION
ISBN 0-9666753-6-3

10 9 8 7 6 5 4 3 2 1

[introduction]

TO SOME PEOPLE, A YARD ISN'T MUCH MORE THAN A NEUTRAL zone separating public from private, an emerald moat that must be crossed en route to the castle. Others denounce their yard as a maintenance headache that throbs every time temperatures creep above freezing. Yet people who love their yard dread time spent away from it. Why such a difference in attitude? Perhaps it has something to do with knowing how to make a yard livable, and being able to keep it that way with minimal effort. *** Though millions know him as the master carpenter of *This Old House*, Norm Abram also has grass to cut and trees to prune in his own yard. Those who know Norm's approach to caring for a house will recognize his yard-care tactic: Prevent problems with regular maintenance. *This Old House* contractor Tom Silva agrees, and puts it this way: "It's a lot easier to prevent problems than it is to solve them later." But a yard is more than a maintenance obligation. A great yard provides contrasts of color and texture that complement the silhouette of a house. It's where the kids play and the family relaxes. In the following chapters, drawn from the pages of *This Old House* magazine, you'll see how Norm, Tom, and other craftsmen add livability to a yard.

—THE EDITORS

[tools and equipment]

WHATEVER the threat, some STUBBORN SOULS STILL USE THEIR BARE hands, preferring MANEUVERABILITY TO ARMOR.

[hand protection]

A GLOVE IS EXPENDABLE SKIN. STONEMASONS, CARPENTERS, electricians, butchers, arborists, firefighters, divers, oyster shuckers, lumberjacks, glassblowers, sheet-metal workers and especially alligator wranglers know that an extra layer of leather, Kevlar or steel mesh can make a big difference.

store gloves *where they can air-dry indoors. Extra pairs let you keep working while wet gloves dry completely.*

Anyone facing a weekend of yardwork may need protection from everything from spiny plants and stinging insects to rough rock and pesticides. The glove must fit the work as well as the worker, and wearing them is often a calculated trade-off between dexterity and safety. "My preference would be not to use them because you don't have as much feedback," says Mark Fitzpatrick, who managed *This Old House*'s Savannah project. "But I'm safety-minded, so I'd rather err on the side of wearing them. On a construction site, there's not much that can't hurt you."

Fitzpatrick has gloves for nearly every task: traditional cowhide and canvas gloves for demolition or any job with an abrasion risk; heavier, cut-proof chain-mail gloves for grinding sharp blades; chemical-protection gloves to handle solvents (each compound has an ideal solvent, and each solvent has a specific glove material to protect against it).

Leather gloves, made from the hide of a cow, pig or goat, are still best for many jobs, providing a true second skin. Cowhide is most common, offering a tough, abrasion-resistant skin over skin. Pigskin is breathable, breaks in nicely and dries soft even when repeatedly wetted. The lanolin in goatskin makes for suppleness, abrasion resistance and tactile sensitivity. Deerskin is good for insulated, cold-weather gloves. For maximum dexterity, glove mavens recommend sheepskin, which also contains lanolin.

Glove-makers divide an animal hide into inner and outer layers. The outer layer, called top grain, is smooth and water-repellent. The inner layer is called *split*. Side split, from over the animal's ribs, is strong and dense. Shoulder split is coarser, stiffer and less expensive.

Whatever the threat, some stubborn souls still use their bare hands, preferring the maneuverability of the sports car to the armor of the tank. Fitzpatrick, having encountered life's dangerous surprises, is not one of them. If you're wearing gloves, he notes, "you don't notice all the times you don't get injured."

This fireproof glove is clumsy, but its silica-based fabric can tolerate temperatures up to 2,000 degrees. That is about 350 degrees hotter than molten iron—just the ticket for lifting hot grates off the barbecue. A number of similarly exotic gloves are available for specialized tasks, but none match the all-round utility of leather.

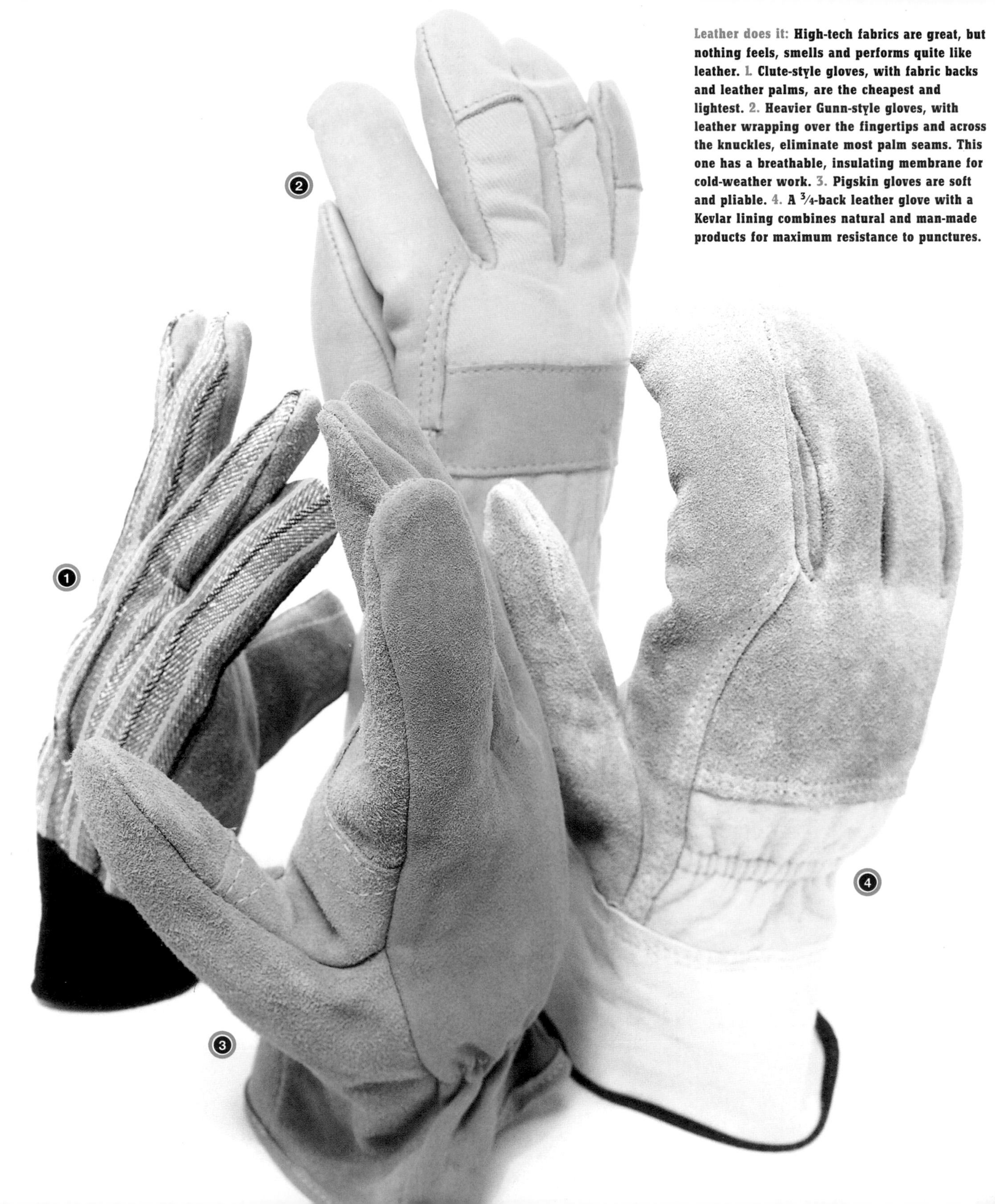

Leather does it: **High-tech fabrics are great, but nothing feels, smells and performs quite like leather. 1. Clute-style gloves, with fabric backs and leather palms, are the cheapest and lightest. 2. Heavier Gunn-style gloves, with leather wrapping over the fingertips and across the knuckles, eliminate most palm seams. This one has a breathable, insulating membrane for cold-weather work. 3. Pigskin gloves are soft and pliable. 4. A ¾-back leather glove with a Kevlar lining combines natural and man-made products for maximum resistance to punctures.**

[pruning tools]

THE BEST SEASON FOR pruning varies by plant. Evergreen shrubs such as yew and juniper should be pruned at the first hint of spring. For shrubs vulnerable to frost, such as rhododendron and azalea, forestry expert Dennis Ryan recommends pruning out dieback—withered branches that won't support new growth—after the snow melts and the ground starts to thaw, thus assuring that water will be available for new growth. Live branches of spring-flowering trees and shrubs should be pruned right after flowering. "Dogwood, flowering cherry, crab apple, rhododendron, azalea and forsythia are ideally pruned immediately after their flowers have withered and dropped off," says Ryan. "Prune too early, and you cut off this year's buds; wait too long, and you'll remove the following spring's buds." Technique aside, here are the tools you'll need.

1. This bow saw, available with blades for both green and seasoned wood, features a knuckle-saving hand guard. 2. In a new take on the combination pole saw and pruner, the rope that controls the shear runs inside the fiberglass handle. 3. The adjustable top blade of a classic bypass shear stays tightly aligned with the lower blade; every part on this lifetime tool is replaceable. 4. A folding saw excels at close work and wherever thick growth stymies big saws; the aggressive 7½-inch blade cuts on the pull. 5. With its 22-inch aluminum handles, the lopper prunes with power and reaches up to high branches and into dense shrubs; it cuts limbs up to 1¼ in. across. 6. Short carbon-steel blades on scissorlike shears allow surgical precision on bonsai and delicate bud ends. 7. Lopping shears are customary for arboreal amputations; this model is made largely of a nylon-fiberglass composite, making it unusually light.

3
4
5
6

[automatic watering]

FOR YEARS, THIS OLD HOUSE GARDENER RUSS MORASH FOUND watering his lawn an aggravating chore: "It was a pain. I had to haul around heavy hoses and hook them to oscillating sprinklers. I was always getting called to the phone—and then I'd wake up in the middle of the night and remember that the sprinklers were still on." Sodden soil didn't help his lawn.

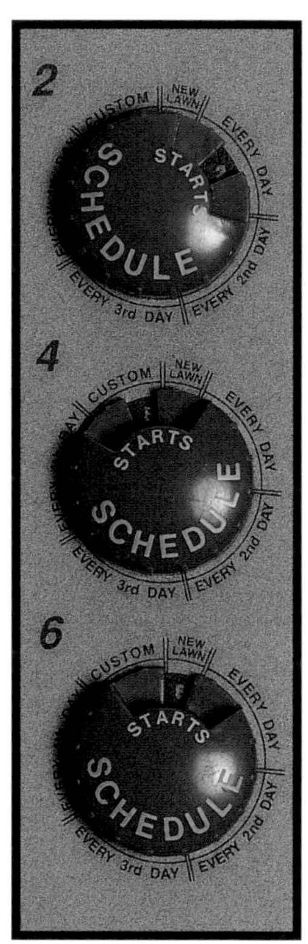

A control panel such as the one above can fully automate an underground sprinkler system. Simpler set-and-forget controllers can time watering from hoses as well.

UNDERGROUND SPRINKLERS

Finally, Russ put in a lawn irrigation system that tends itself. The underground sprinklers switch on automatically when the soil is dry, pop up and deliver just the right amount of water, then click off and disappear until needed again. The system saves water because the sprinklers cycle on in the early morning when evaporation is less of a problem. And the lawn stays healthier because there's plenty of time for the grass blades to dry by nightfall.

Planning a system is less daunting than it may first appear. Stores that sell parts often give away fliers with good step-by-step instructions. Some manufacturers offer free design services, and you may even find layout grids and detailed instructions on company Web sites. One note of caution: Some published directions give short shrift to what needs to be done to prevent ice damage and to keep water in the sprinkler system from siphoning back into household water. Requirements for dealing with both of these problems vary by region; a local parts-supply store or landscaper can provide more specifics.

The biggest decisions are how to group the sprinklers and what type of heads to use. "Put sprinklers that will be in the sun on one circuit, those in the shade on another," advises *This Old House* landscaper Roger Cook. That way, sprinklers can be left on longer where more water is needed. Each circuit can contain only one type of sprinkler head. Bubblers, which deliver a softly flowing gurgle of water, work great for roses or other plants with foliage that shouldn't get wet. For lawns less than 15 feet across, the only choice is the basic sprayer, which waters in a fixed pattern. For large areas, impact heads or rotor heads work better. With a reach of 15 to 60 feet, they can often be placed just outside the lawn, easing installation and eliminating the danger of snapping off a sprinkler head with a lawn mower. Rotors—also called gear-drive heads—vary the throw of water, require less maintenance, and spread more evenly than impact sprayers, which go pip, pip, pip as an arm rhythmically breaks up a jet of water. "The advantage of rotors is that all the parts are enclosed, so they stay free of grit and

After Russ put in an underground lawn irrigation system, he no longer needed surface sprinklers. Not only did he save a lot of hose-lugging, but he also improved the accuracy of watering coverage. Setting up a permanent system once means that you don't have to scrutinize the coverage each time you turn the water on.

[automatic watering]

TECHNIQUES

Once the plan was complete, it took just a few hours to get Russ's underground sprinklers into action.

1 **Roger Cook tapped into a pipeline from Russ's well. On the black pipe leading up from the ground, he installed a valve that can be connected to an air compressor to blow the system free of water. Above that is a pressure vacuum breaker that local water officials require to prevent sprinkler water from siphoning back into the well. The device must be at least a foot higher than all sprinkler heads, so Cook put it next to other ugly utility services on a wall of Russ's workshop.**

2 **In a trench about 10 inches deep, Cook laid high-pressure Schedule 40 PVC pipe leading to a round box that shelters valves for the sprinkler circuits. The pipe connections were easy—Cook just glued them together. He buried the box so its cover lies at ground level.**

3 **With a pipe-pulling machine secured from a rental yard, Cook put the rest of the irrigation lines into place. The machine sliced through the sod, leaving only a thin trail of loose dirt to show where the flexible tubing lay. Tubing is adequate for individual circuits, where water pressure is low, but rigid pipe must be used on the high-pressure line leading to the valves.**

4 **Cook connected the sprinklers with another type of flexible tubing instead of rigid risers, which are more likely to snap and harder to position precisely. He set each sprinkler so the top of the head was level with the surface of the soil. "If you set the heads up too high, the lawn mower comes across and eats them," he says.**

sand," says Mike Struhs of Rain Bird Sales of Azuza, California. "What a lot of people like about impact sprinklers, though, is the sound. If properly placed, there is no major difference in how evenly the two kinds spray."

Compared with how long Russ wished for automatic sprinklers, the installation itself was lightning-quick. Cook began digging the trench for the main pipe about 8 a.m., carefully shoveling the dirt onto burlap laid next to the lawn to keep the grass free of mud. Then he powered up a pipe-pulling machine

Cook adjusts the arc of one sprinkler so that the spray reaches the heads of adjacent sprinklers. Head-to-head coverage helps ensure even watering.

[automatic watering]

and yanked the tubing into place across the main expanse of lawn. "Without the trencher, we'd still be digging," Cook said as he sat down to sip iced tea at 1:30 p.m. Then he was back on his feet. Although he had not yet installed the sprinkler heads, he turned water on to one circuit at a time to flush out debris. "The biggest factor is dirt, but pebbles can be in there too," says Gary Capstick (of Turf Products Corp. of Massachusetts), who helped with the job. Cook attached the heads, checked the spray to make sure all areas were being watered evenly, and shoveled soil back into the trench. By late afternoon, he was packing up his tools, and the yard was ready for entertaining.

"Even though this lawn has the deepest and best soil on my property, it goes into decline if it's not watered regularly," Russ says. "We can't have that."

keep spares *on hand. If a fixture or fitting fails, and cleaning doesn't help it, replacement might be called for.*

DRIP IRRIGATION

Sprinklers serve lawns well, but inexpensive drip irrigation often works better for everything else. Drip systems save water by giving each plant precisely the water it needs. Leaves remain dry (so plants stay healthier), weeds wither, and some gardeners even report far fewer snails. Developed in Israel in the 1960s, drip systems consist of controls, distribution tubing, and emitters that dispense the water (right). Installation is easy; all that's required is a utility knife and a hole punch. Tubing can lie on the surface or be hidden under a layer of mulch.

When designing a yard-size system, begin by assessing plant needs, not how the yard is laid out. Drip tubing is inexpensive, so you can put plants that need frequent water into one zone and those that need less water into another, regardless of where the plants are. When the piping as been laid out, decide how much water each plant needs per irrigation. Emitters deliver a specific number of gallons per hour, but if this rating isn't meaningful, think in terms of multiples: Plant A needs one dose of water; Plant B needs twice as much. For Plant B, you can either buy a bigger-capacity emitter or install twice as many. Large plants benefit from having more emitters because a wider area of soil is moistened. Finally, calculate whether your water pressure will support all the emitters that you want to use at once—instructions are available where supplies are sold. If not, create more zones.

Drip systems are relatively trouble-free. Where winters are cold, disconnect the water supply each fall and remove the end cap. If this doesn't drain tubing, blow out the water with compressed air or walk the system from the faucet to the end, lifting the tubing as you go (a little remaining water won't hurt). During the growing season, check periodically for wilted plants (a sign of clogged emitters), or soggy ground (a signal that the tubing has been cut). If poking with a pin doesn't open a clogged emitter, insert a new one nearby. Splice around any cracks in the tubing. As plants mature, adjust the system by adding emitters or replacing some with plugs. In many cases, drip irrigation will get bushes and trees off to such a robust start that they can take care of themselves after a few years.

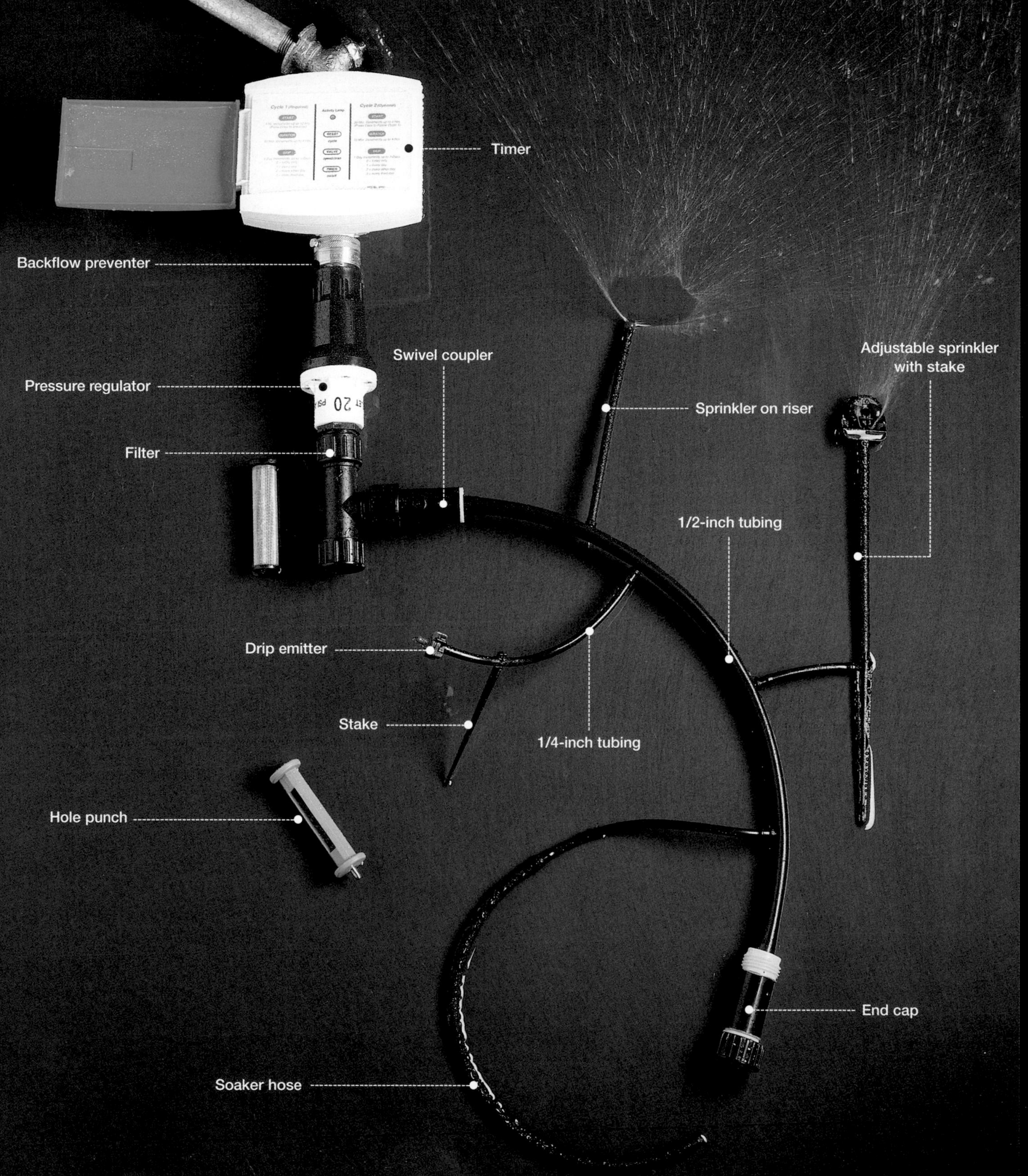

Timer
Backflow preventer
Swivel coupler
Pressure regulator
Sprinkler on riser
Adjustable sprinkler with stake
Filter
1/2-inch tubing
Drip emitter
Stake
1/4-inch tubing
Hole punch
End cap
Soaker hose

[earth movers]

THE TYPICAL GARDEN runs on wheels. For every plant that grows, it seems, there are rocks to move, fertilizer to lug, and waste to trundle away. If horticulture predated the wheel, it wasn't by much. Ancestors of the homely one-wheel cart—the wheelbarrow—must surely have rolled down Roman roads. *This Old House* executive producer (and avid gardener) Russ Morash relies on the traditional single-wheel wheelbarrow. "It's unstable, it's tough on your back, and you can't tilt it down to pick up heavy objects," he says. "But it still can't be beat when you have a narrow path to navigate." A wheelbarrow, though, isn't the only versatile mover that's good in a garden.

THE BOBCAT

It is not yardwork bliss to face a mountain of loam or several tons of gravel armed with a shovel and wheelbarrow; it is backbreaking, spirit-crushing torture. Good thing there's relief at the rental yard, where you'll find a miniature, layman-friendly earth-mover called the Bobcat. It is one of several brands of skid-steer machines that work like tanks: Instead of a steering wheel, there are levers on either side of the cabin. Push both forward, you go forward; pull them back, you go in reverse. Push one forward and pull the other back, you spin in place. Pivoting foot pedals control the lift arm and bucket. The vehicle can scoop up great heaps of material yet maneuver around obstructions like a ballerina. Accessories—augers, tillers, backhoes, pallet forks, graders, rakes, breakers (hefty jackhammers), trench-diggers, and snowblowers—are secured by a pair of levers. "We used two of these critters," says Russ, "to put in 10,000 square feet of new lawn. They rototilled, moved dump-truck loads of soil, and raked it out smooth without any hand labor. We were done in 2½ hours."

Time to load, lug or spread? A shovel (far left) moves little loads with gusto; 12-gauge steel blades won't flex or crack as readily as thinner metal. A Bobcat (left) saves time on the big jobs, but even such a deft hauler can't outmaneuver Russ (right) and his trusty wheelbarrow.

[earth movers]

English spades, the gardener's gold standard, have unbreakable forged-steel blades that cut roots, pry up rocks, and can withstand a firm stomp on the step. Tradition calls for short shafts of stout hickory or ash topped with a D- or T-handle. But you'll need more than a good spade in most gardens.

Renting a skid-steer loader is actually less difficult than renting a car. Some states don't even require a driver's license. Many rental agents will demonstrate the machine for you, and some have a basic instructional video.

SHOVELS

There are seemingly infinite variations of the shovel, but the most common question seems to be this: What is the difference between a spade and a shovel? A shovel blade is often heart-shaped, to cut deeply, and almost always concave. A spade's blade is usually square and flatter. There are, however, curvy spades and flattish shovels.

Shovel handles are mainly 2-feet long with a D-shaped end, or 4 feet long with a knobbed end. Scoop shovels have the shorter handle, best for lifting loose material such as grain or sand. Long handles give extra leverage for breaking sod. Traditionally, handles are turned from ash or hickory, but wood is susceptible to weathering and rot, especially at the socket. Fiberglass handles are making reluctant converts out of those who love the feel of wood but not the sound of handles snapping.

Using any shovel all day will make your back sore all night—if not forever. The human spinal column was not designed to twist and torque repetitively under heavy load, and a decent self-regard requires attention to form:

RABBITING

FORGED

DRAIN

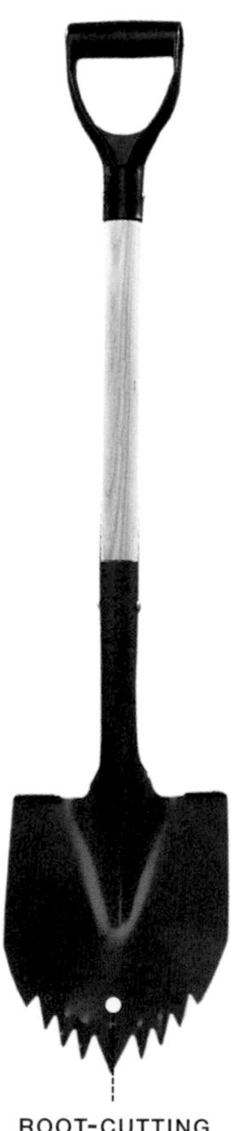

ROOT-CUTTING

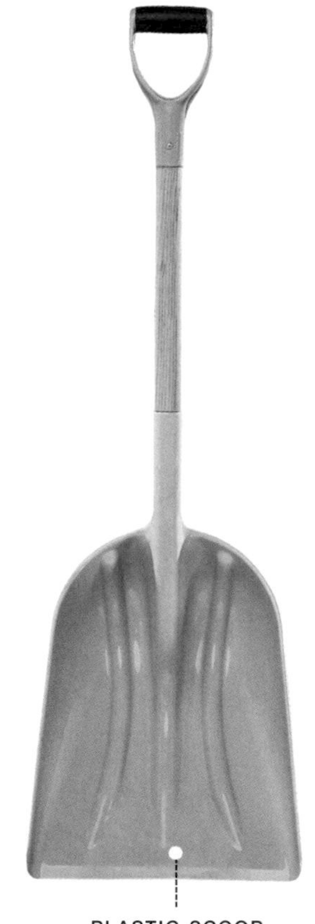

PLASTIC SCOOP

EMERGENCY

Take frequent breaks and small bites (never more than five pounds); position the wheelbarrow so you don't have to turn to fill it; and avoid abrupt or violent movement. Expert shovelers work slowly and patiently, like a sexton. Do thou likewise.

Shovels should get periodic honings with a flat mill file on the inside bevel: not razor-sharp, just a clearly defined edge. How often you hone depends on how much you work. At the end of every job, spray them with oil and store them indoors. Once a year, offer wooden handles a coat of boiled linseed oil. Fiberglass-handled shovels can be stored out of the weather and kept clean but otherwise ignored.

WHEELBARROWS

"If I could have only one carrier," Russ says, "I'd make it a wheelbarrow. But it would have to be big enough—a capacity of at least a third of a cubic yard. A too-small wheelbarrow is of no use." Russ also has a two-wheel garden cart, the kind with bicycle-type wheels and sides of exterior-grade plywood. "These are great for hauling bulky debris," he says.

Then there's his two-wheel hand truck, the kind used for hoisting refrigerators. With its easy fulcrum and low center of gravity, a hand truck can transport fence sections, bags of lime or cement, rocks, or just about any item that would be tough to muscle into a carrier.

Ergonomic studies show that using a long handle and the lightest shovel can lessen back strain. Most shovels weigh about 4 to 5 pounds. Blades come in two basic types: round points for piercing soil and square points for moving loose materials.

NONSPARKING

FLUTED-EDGE

LONG-HANDLED

ROUND-POINT

SIFTING

ALUMINUM SQUARE-POINT

[lawn mowers]

IT IS EARLY SATURDAY morning, and you've just spent 20 minutes trying to kick 40 pounds of mulish lawn mower into self-sustaining activity. Your reward? A nerve-jangling hour of mowing enveloped in a cocoon of oily vapors and deafening engine noise. Perhaps you should learn to take better care of the mower that tortures you. Or maybe you need a new mower.

any mower *should be stored under cover when not in use. A waterproof tarp will work, but a garage or storage building is better.*

PUSH MOWERS

Indeed, you could be walking behind a mower that consumes neither gas nor electricity, starts instantly and is so quiet that you can almost eavesdrop on the neighbors.

The wonderful implement is a push-reel mower, invented in 1830 as a mechanized alternative to sheep and scythes. Even now, the spinning reel with fixed cutter bar remains the ne plus ultra of grass clippers. Unlike rotary power mowers, which flay off grass tips, leaving ragged wounds that turn gray, reel mowers snip grass as neatly as scissors cut hair. "Grass seems to grow denser and fluffier when cut with a reel," says George Toma, a former head groundskeeper for the Kansas City Royals who fondly remembers cutting baseball infields with push mowers.

They're great for lawns under a quarter of an acre, though a good one can cost as much as a decent gas mower. Reel mowers can be either self-sharpening (their blades touch the cutter bar) or silent (blades clear the bar within three-thousandths of an inch).

The reel mower's chief drawback is poor performance in tall grass. At the height of the growing season, you're either out there every eight days or you're borrowing a gas mower. And although three inches is the recommended cutting height for many lawns, most reels go no higher than 2¼ inches. But maintenance is minimal: a quick brushing to clear clippings, a spray of oil to stop blade rust, and a sharpening every three years or so.

POWER MOWERS

Gasoline mowers, which cut most of the lawns in this country, produce 2 to 5 percent of our air pollution—astounding when you consider how little they're used. Their inefficient, cheap engines can emit as many hydrocarbons in one hour as a new car does in 344 miles. National emission standards for new models stiffened in 1999, but even the cleanest gas mowers will still be very dirty. What's the alternative? Some suggest electric mowers. But they are either tied to extension cords or depend on battery power, which poses a disposal problem.

Small, well-tended lawns cut easily on human power alone. But power mowers work better on large lawns, or lawns of any size that go too long between trimmings. To finish the job in an hour, choose a walk-behind model for a lawn of less than a quarter-acre, and a

When power mowers conquered suburbia in the 1950s, reel sales slipped, and those who grew up pushing reels were glad to be rid of them. But modern reels are at least a third lighter than the old cast-iron behemoths, and some models have slippery nylon gearing instead of rust-prone metal.

[lawn mowers]

ride-on for a lawn of more than a half-acre. For a mid-size lawn, the decision depends on complexity of the landscape. Walk-behinds easily cut into corners and around flower beds. Ride-ons excel in open expanses, trimming up to 42 inches in a swath, double the path of walk-behinds. Rear-engine riding mowers are more nimble than lawn tractors, making them a good choice for not-too-big lawns with turns and twists. The decision has financial implications, too. Manual mowers cost $100 to $300. Walk-behind power mulchers range from $150 to $800. Electric models are quietest; get one with a rechargeable battery, not a cord. Rear-engine riders are $600 to $2,500. Lawn tractors: $700 to $4,000.

Mulching mowers save time because there's no need to rake or empty bags of clippings. They also save at least part of the expense and effort of adding separate fertilizer, because the clippings are rich in nitrogen. (Some experts say clippings provide half the nitrogen a lawn needs.) It's possible to get the same benefits with a standard mower simply by leaving the clippings, but because non-mulchers don't shred the grass blades as thoroughly, the clippings are in bigger pieces and thus more obvious for a day or two. Side-discharge mowers tend to send the clippings flying if the bagger isn't on, spreading the debris into adjacent flower beds. Mulchers deposit the clippings right in the mower's path.

LAWN MOWER CARE

By summer's end, you've no doubt marched countless steps behind your trusty lawn mower. With fall comes the time to put Old Faithful away. Most likely, your workhorse is a walk-behind deck with a four-cycle engine; some 35 million of these beasts ramble over American lawns. The best maintenance for this lawn mower is a thorough cleaning and an oil change. Also, remember to tighten every bolt you can find, replace the spark plug and air filter, and sharpen the blade (don't forget to precisely balance it afterward) or replace it.

A riding mower needs much the same care as other power mowers. But in addition, clean and lubricate choke and throttle linkages, change the engine and transaxle oils, check the muffler for corrosion, replace worn drive belts and pulley bearings, tighten loose belts, remove the mower deck to scrape off grass, and place the tractor on wood blocks so its wheels hang free.

1. Squeeze fuel stabilizer into the mower's gas tank, then drain the fuel in one of two ways: Run the tank dry while giving the lawn its final cut of the season, or siphon the fuel into a gas can. (Be careful not to spill gas; when it evaporates it releases polluting hydrocarbons.) Restart the engine until it won't start. This removes remaining fuel, protecting the tank and carburetor from condensation and rust. 2. Remove the spark plug as a safety measure, then loosen the crankcase plug, drain the oil into a drip pan and take the used oil to a recycling station. 3. Now turn the mower on its side and scrape away grass and mud buildup on the deck and blades, using a putty knife. After cleaning, protect bare steel parts of the mower deck with a light coat of household oil. Grass, mud and other gunk in the cooling fins can make an air-cooled engine overheat. Clean between the fins with an ice-cream stick or any scrap of wood that slides easily into the slits. Replace the air filter, check the owner's manual for any additional maintenance steps and, finally, roll your trusty sidekick into the shed for its winter snooze. 4. Drop a few teaspoons of engine oil into the spark plug's empty hole, and pull the starter rope to turn the engine over and distribute the oil. Install a new plug, but for the sake of safety, leave the wire off until spring.

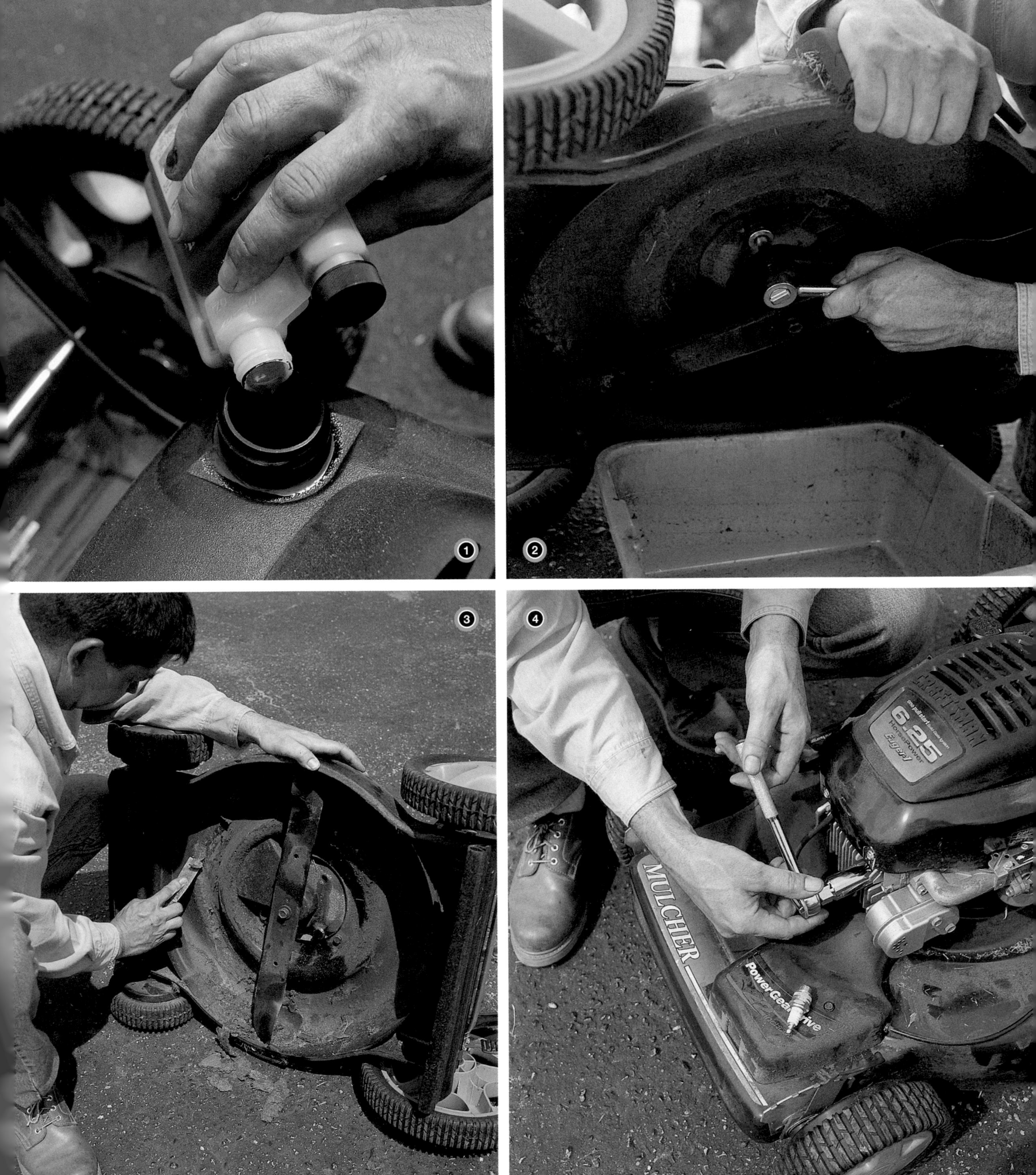
1
2
3
4
6.25
HorsePower
MULCHER

[yard cleanup tools]

THE SAPLINGS LIE WHERE YOU CUT THEM—WAS IT LAST summer or the one before? Behind the woodshed are stacks of raspberry canes, torn out when you refurbished the garden. All these heaps of surplus cellulose can be turned into mulch—brown gold—if you can collect them.

CHIPPER-SHREDDERS

Cross a food processor with a trash compactor. Then think in terms of all outdoors. That's the idea behind chipper-shredders. These gasoline-powered machines greatly reduce the volume of garden and tree debris by regurgitating it as mulch (*left*). More mobile than commercial chippers, chipper-shredders have their own engines and seldom pack more than 10 horsepower. The mechanism that does the chipping is a rotating steel disk with one or more blades projecting at a slight angle, like the cutting edge of an oversize cheese-slicer. When a branch—with a diameter as large as 3½ inches—goes into the feeder, the blades simultaneously draw the wood in and whack it into ½- to 1-inch chips. A separate hopper feeds the shredder, which thrashes leaves, twigs, light plant material and organic kitchen waste with blades or swinging hammer flails, or a combination of both. The shredder then forces the ground material through a screen or bar grate. The resulting product is deposited

the magic of mulch

THE BIG PAYOFF OF A CHIPPER-SHREDDER IS THE FINAL PRODUCT: FRESH MULCH. A LAYER OF MULCH SPREAD 3 OR 4 INCHES DEEP AROUND PERENNIALS OR TREES—STARTING 6 INCHES FROM THE TRUNK—HELPS RETAIN MOISTURE, PREVENTS EROSION AND REDUCES THE NUMBER OF WEEDS. A THICKER LAYER, 6 TO 8 INCHES DEEP, WILL CONVERT A WEED PATCH INTO A FERTILE FLOWER BED OR VEGETABLE PATCH.

VIRTUALLY ANY FRESH MULCH CAN BE USED ANYWHERE IN THE GARDEN, THOUGH IT CAN TEMPORARILY REDUCE THE NITROGEN AVAILABLE TO PLANTS, PARTICULARLY IF DUG INTO THE SOIL. SPREADING 5-10-5 OR 5-10-10 FERTILIZER ON ESTABLISHED BEDS BEFORE MULCHING CAN MINIMIZE THIS PROBLEM.

A chipper-shredder can be an outstanding yard cleanup partner, but any machine capable of chewing through wood this thick commands respect and caution. Leather gloves and safety glasses are essential. The pros often wear ear muffs: Hearing protection is well advised.

[yard cleanup tools]

With so many rakes available, choosing the right one might seem impossible. Start by realizing that no single rake does all jobs well—you'll need several rakes to manage a typical yard.

into in a cloth collection bag, or dumped directly on the ground.

Differences in horsepower are important when chipping is the primary function. A chipper powered by a 5-horsepower engine takes twice as long as an 8-horsepower engine to devour a branch 2 or 3 inches in diameter. That's no big deal—until you have to clean up after a big ice storm. Chipping blades should be made of hardened tool steel for durability, and they should be easy to remove for sharpening. The more cutting surfaces, the better the machine will work.

RAKES

The show starts when the leaves turn. They glow and flutter in the sharpening air, radiating the sense that this is surely the best of all seasons. Of course, as each leaf hits the ground, anxiety builds about the chore ahead. Raking leaves is hard work, but the very act of uncovering pristine green beneath a riot of red and yellow is satisfying, and the steady repetition of pulling tines across turf frees the mind. In the end, one little patch of the universe is back in order. If that doesn't leave you smiling, maybe you need better tools.

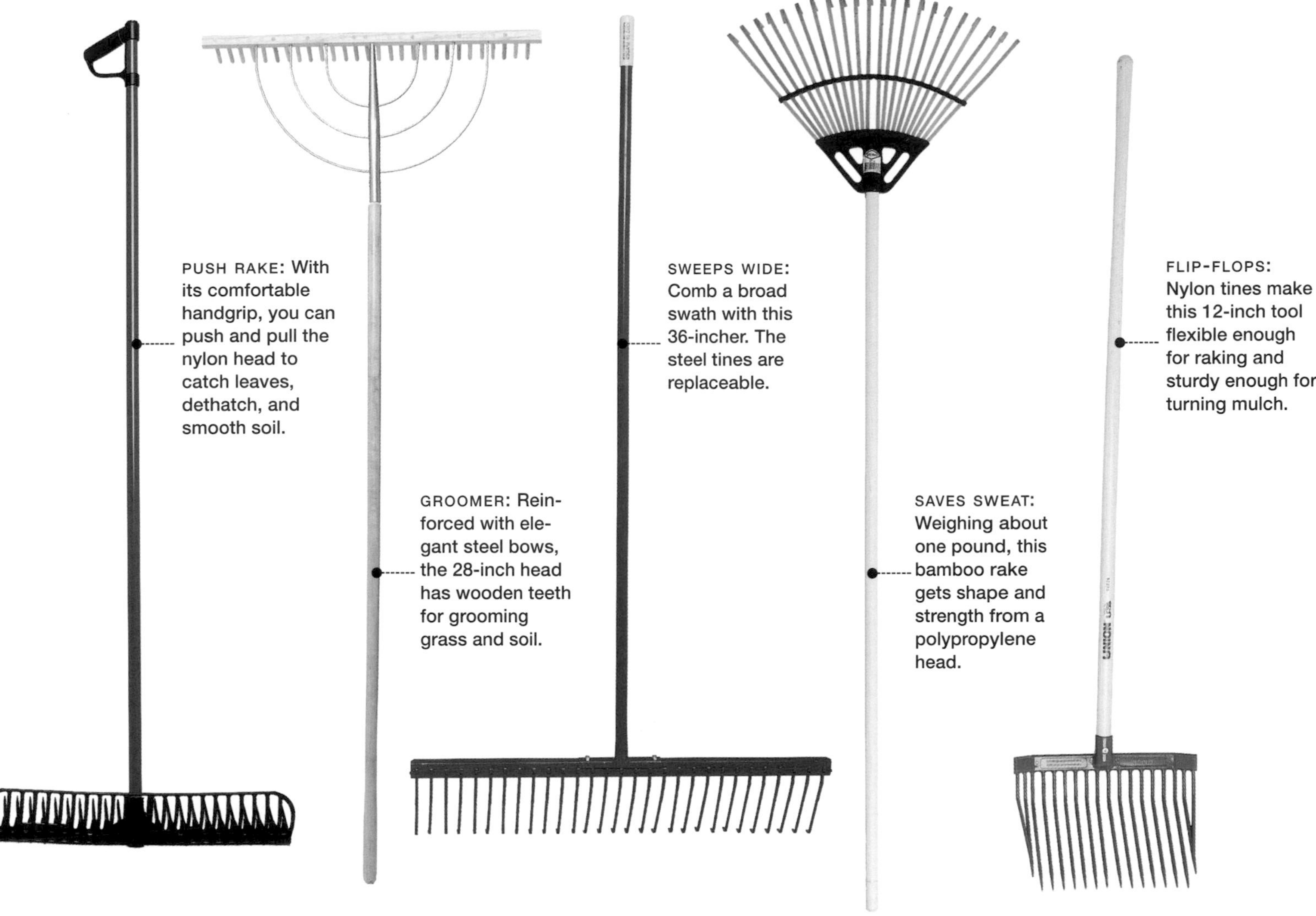

watch where you stick your fingers

START UP A CHIPPER-SHREDDER, AND IT BURSTS INTO VIOLENT, NOISY, VIBRATING ACTION. EAR PROTECTORS, GOGGLES, AND HEAVY GLOVES SHOULD ALWAYS BE WORN WHEN OPERATING A SUCH A TOOL. AND BE SURE TO FASTEN THE GLOVES TIGHTLY: GAUNTLET-STYLE GLOVES CAN EASILY GET SNAGGED ON A BRANCH AND PULLED INTO THE BLADES. THE SAME IS TRUE OF LOOSE CLOTHING. "ONCE YOUR CLOTHING GETS CAUGHT, IN GOES THE ARM," SAYS RUSS MORASH.

THE KEY TO SAFETY, SAYS TOM SILVA, IS TO SLOW DOWN YOUR MOVEMENTS AND FEED MATERIAL GINGERLY. LET GO OF THE WOOD AS SOON AS IT'S IN THE FEEDER POSITION—SO A HAND DOESN'T FOLLOW. "MAKE SURE THAT NO BRANCHES ARE STICKING OUT 90 DEGREES THAT'LL COME DOWN AND WHACK YOU ON THE SIDE OF THE HEAD," TOM SAYS. "KEEP IT STRAIGHT, AND DON'T OVERSIZE THE PIECE FOR THE MACHINE. AND NEVER PUT YOUR HAND DOWN INSIDE A CHIPPER TO CLEAN IT OUT." NEVER. IF YOU MUST UNCLOG A JAM, FIRST REMOVE THE SPARK-PLUG WIRE FROM THE CHIPPER'S ENGINE. EVEN IF YOU HAVE TURNED THE ENGINE OFF, AN IMPELLER UNDER TENSION CAN SHOOT BACK AND SNIP OFF A FINGER.

[string trimmers]

AT THE EDGE OF a lush, green and—almost—perfectly groomed lawn, landscaper Roger Cook yanks the starting cord of a 15-inch handheld line-trimmer, fiddles with the choke, gooses the trigger and marches off to attack a few renegade patches of grass that his lawn tractor missed. Locking in on his targets, Cook buzzes grassy fringes sprouting near rock walls and wisps of grass that ring the trees. The trimmer is an obnoxious critter—noisy and noisome, spewing bits of green in every direction—but no other tool details a freshly cut lawn faster.

Using a string trimmer, says landscaping expert Roger Cook, is like a "dance outdoors with an elegant partner."

Known by a number of aliases—rotary trimmer, weed-trimmer, nylon-line trimmer—a typical string trimmer consists of a hollow metal baton with a sputtering two-cycle engine at one end and a fast-spinning plastic hub at the other. Inside the baton is a steel driveshaft or flexible cable. The sealed hub contains anywhere from 25 to 75 feet of stout nylon or copolymer line. When the trimmer is at rest, a couple of 4-inch strands curl out from the hub like cowlicks. Once the head starts spinning at about 8,000 revolutions per minute, the strands straighten out into ruthless plant assassins. The whirling strings annihilate weedy plots and dig out pesky growth in the cracks of flagstone walkways. With the right accessory, a simple trimmer can even till the earth, throw snow or slice saplings to the ground.

GEAR HOUSING

CUTTER HEAD OR HUB

NYLON LINE

DEBRIS SHIELD

A typical trimmer. A string trimmer consists of a hollow metal baton with a sputtering two-cycle engine at one end and a fast-spinning plastic hub at the other. Inside the baton is a steel driveshaft or flexible cable. Split-boom trimmers can accommodate accessories such as chainsaw bars, hedge pruners, and even snow-throwers.

POWER HEAD. Contains the engine, clutch, and fuel system.

STARTER HANDLE.

AIR CLEANER. Prevents dirt and debris from entering engine. Clean frequently.

LOOP HANDLE. Allows a good grip no matter which way the trimmer is turned.

GRIP. Cushioned to dampen vibrations.

RUN/STOP SWITCH. Stops the engine instantly; an important safety feature.

THROTTLE TRIGGER. Controls the speed of the trimmer.

FUEL TANK. For gas/oil mix. Fuel level should be visible through tank walls.

BOOM. Contains the driveshaft or drive cable.

1. Electric trimmer. A curved-shaft electric trimmer is quiet and light, but the need for a power cord limits its range. Best for light duty close to the house. 2. Brush cutter. A brush cutter has a toothy steel blade in place of string, and cuts very aggressively. It can cut down 3-inch saplings or woody vines at grade level, without leaving a stump. The tool demands particular vigilance during use. 3. Split-shaft trimmer. A knob on the boom of a split-shaft string trimmer makes it easy to replace the head with seasonal accessories. The shield on a trimmer's hub deflects flying debris. 4. Four-cycle trimmer. This trimmer emits fewer hydrocarbons and has more torque than a trimmer with a two-cycle engine. The J handle reverses for either left- or right-handed use.

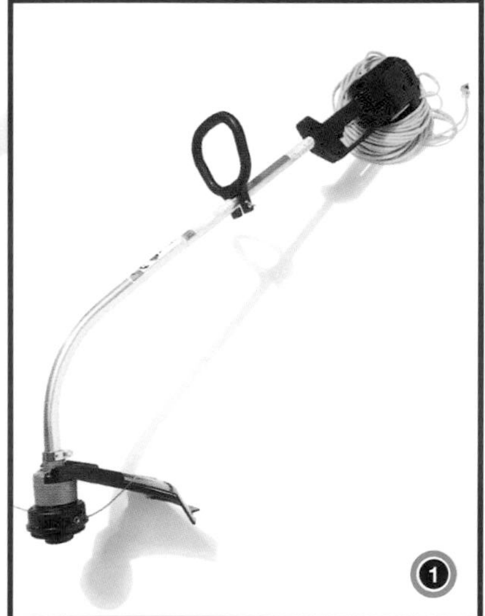

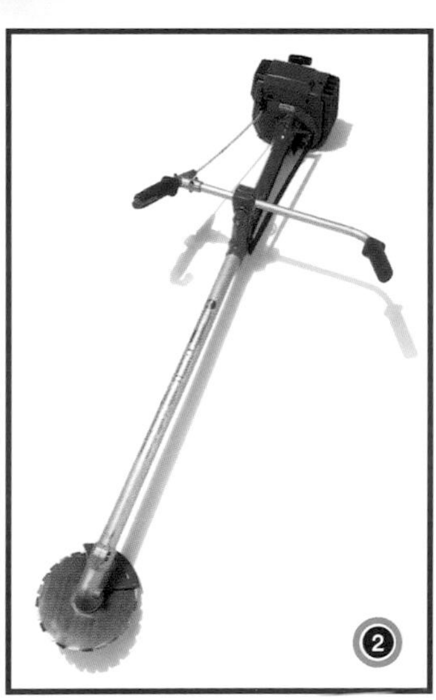

[string trimmers]

As Cook continues his search-and-destroy mission, he concentrates on the blurry orange halo at the end of the tool. Moving up to 600 feet per second, the tip of the line cuts best, but Cook takes care not to cut lower than a lawn mower would. "If you look at where you've been and see a narrow swath of grass that's a slightly different color than what's next to it, you've scalped the lawn," he says. Scalping makes turf vulnerable to disease and dehydration in hot weather, not to mention making a lawn look pathetic. To avoid buzz-cutting, Cook keeps the hub level. He is especially dainty around tree trunks because repeatedly scoring the bark can kill even a fairly large tree.

String trimmers can be cantankerous and unpredictable, but the tool's mulish disposition usually results from poor care and misunderstanding. Just as a cheap blade can slow a good power saw, a mediocre hub can hamper a string trimmer. The best hubs are made of fiberglass-reinforced polycarbonate. Most hubs have a bump-button on the bottom, which wears out after a season or two of everyday use. Periodically taking a break from trimming to tap the bump-button releases an inch or so of line to replace what has worn off. A metal edge slices off any excess once the head resumes spinning.

Heads that don't feed string properly have exasperated so many users that some manufacturers are replacing spool heads with fixed-line heads: a simple disk that holds two short strands of line that can be easily replaced when they wear out.

Even with a perfectly maintained trimmer, Cook advises taking special safety precautions. He scouts brushy areas and deep grass before he trims—just as he sizes up a tree before cutting it. Hazards such as stone, brick, cement and glass always pop up where least expected. (Glass sprays like shrapnel when a brush-cutter blade hits it.) But whipped into an eye at high speed, even a slender blade of grass can slice delicate tissue. Eye protection, therefore, is an "absolute must," says Cook—as is ear protection. One of his biggest fears, however, is yellow jackets. "Hit a nest," he says, "and you'll have the whole hive up and at you in about 30 seconds." What then? "Get out of Dodge."

A clogged air filter will choke an engine dead. After four hours of trimming, remove the filter, rinse it in soapy water, dry and reinstall.

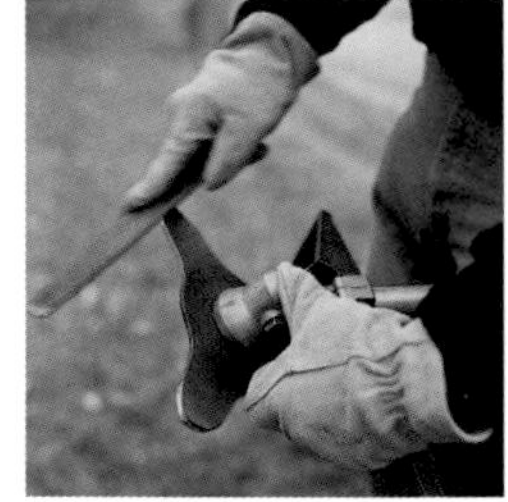

Some trimmers can be fitted with a stiff blade to cut brush. If it dulls, sharpen the cutting edges with a flat file. If the blade is bent, replace it.

When rewinding heads, keep coils snug and parallel; loose coils chafe against each other, and the heat of friction can fuse the string to itself.

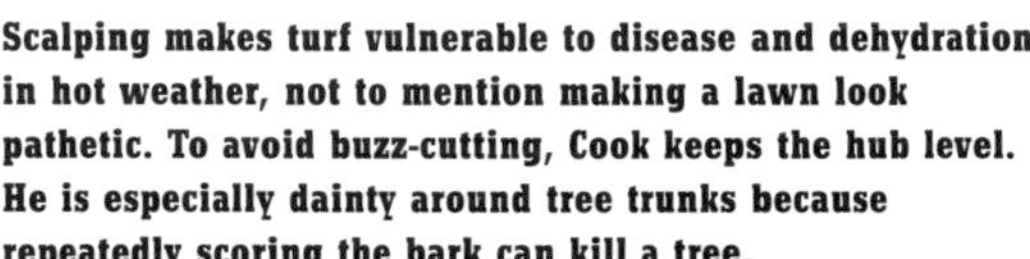

Scalping makes turf vulnerable to disease and dehydration in hot weather, not to mention making a lawn look pathetic. To avoid buzz-cutting, Cook keeps the hub level. He is especially dainty around tree trunks because repeatedly scoring the bark can kill a tree.

Cook trims encroaching grass near walkways by tipping his string trimmer up on edge. The cut takes practice, however, because the string kicks up dirt if it dips too low. This kind of trimming calls for a firm grip and a steady gait, with elbows held close to the body so that only the tip of the line touches the grass. It also calls for safety glasses or, even better, a face shield. Be sure to warn bystanders to keep well out of the way, too.

CLEAR the site of EXISTING VEGETATION.

PREPARE SOIL: ROTOTILL, RAKE TO REMOVE ROCKS/DEBRIS, AMEND soil, rake, firm SOIL.

[the new lawn]

A DOOR, A WINDOW, A red brick chimney with its curling, skyward-bound wisp of smoke...these are the familiar icons of "house" depicted in a thousand children's drawings. And when the ideal is embellished with crayoned landscaping, what often appears is a broad swath of deep-green, toe-tickling, cushiony grass. For most kids, maybe even most adults, a lawn is one of the hallmarks of home. Little wonder, then, that so many spend so much to get it. Fall is the best time to plant a new lawn, but preparation can begin earlier.

Creating a lush carpet of grass where only dirt exists calls for a good bit of imagination, but even more important: thorough soil preparation and the right seeding technique.

Soil preparation is a crucial step in getting ready for any new lawn. Some landscapers recommend killing existing vegetation with the herbicide glyphosate (the active ingredient in Roundup), which is said to be of low residual toxicity. For a chemical-free yard, however, cover the area with black plastic for a few weeks to let the sun bake what's below, or follow the lead of *This Old House* landscaper Roger Cook. "I use a sod-cutting machine to remove lawn, and then I toss the material into a compost pile," he says. "That eliminates grassy clumps left by other methods." Meanwhile, send a soil sample to the county extension service; they will return a detailed list of minerals and organic matter that you'll need to add later. Once the grass is gone, rototill in a thick layer of organic material (leaf mold, rotted manure or other compost) as grass food, along with any amendments suggested by the soil test. Cook, for example, tills in an inch or two of course sand to loosen clay soils. Rake the area to remove rocks and

A tidy house floating on a sea of green...to many, this is the only combination that can truly be considered "home."

[the new lawn]

1. **Hydromulch is made from ground newspaper or shredded wood fiber, or a combination of the two. The mulch is dyed green to help the applicater see which areas have been covered.**
2. **Seed (or a blend of several kinds of seeds) and enough fertilizer to carry the planting through its first month are the other principal ingredients of hydroseed. Landscapers usually mix these elements with the mulch and water for a one-shot application.**
3. **The mix is applied by sprayer hose as a uniform ¾-inch blanket over the entire area to be planted. Because the water is already mixed in, the area does not need to be watered for at least a day. The thick mulch also helps to suppress weeds until the tiny seeds are well on their way.**

debris, and to even out the surface. Finally, firm up the soil with a lawn roller and fill in low spots.

HANDSEEDING AND SOD

The two most common ways to turn prepared soil into a lush green carpet represent the extremes of expense and patience. Sprinkling seeds over the ground is inexpensive, but you'll have to wait at least two weeks for the seeds to germinate and several more before the area even begins to resemble a lawn.

You can seed bare spots by hand, but an area larger than a few hundred square feet calls for a drop spreader or a broadcast spreader. Make two passes at right angles to each other in order to even the application, but don't waste seed: Spreading more than the seed bag instructions call for won't make a lawn fill in any faster or grow any better. ("And use this year's seed," says Cook. Last year's seed might seem a bargain, but may not germinate properly.) Lightly rake the area, then use a drum roller to press seeds into the soil. Finally, spread a light covering of clean straw over the area to retain moisture, then water it lightly twice each day. When the grass is about 2½ inches high, gently rake off the hay and mow your new lawn for the first time.

"If you don't want to invest your time in seeding a lawn," says Cook, "invest in sod." You can go from bare dirt to lavish lawn in a single day, just by rolling out these pre-grown lengths of lawn. Sod comes in several grades and with various grasses; what you can get depends on your local suppliers. Prepare the area just as you would for seed, and be sure to water just as carefully.

HYDROSEEDING

One very efficient way to install a new lawn is a method called hydroseeding. The process blends seed, starter fertilizer, water, and green-dyed, ground newsprint or wood fiber into an

oatmeal-like glop that can be sprayed onto the ground. Developed first to heal road cuts along highways, hydroseeding is now used on areas as small as 3,000 square feet because it's fast and effective. Protected by the fiber pulp, new seed needs less water. Seeding wet areas or steep slopes is no longer troublesome, and neither are hungry, seed-stealing birds, who find the cellulose layer a significant deterrent.

The cost of hydroseeding is reasonable, says Sean Bilodeau, a landscaper who once demonstrated the process on a *This Old House* project. Though slightly more expensive than hand seeding, it is far less expensive than sod.

Several companies sell bags of fiber mulch mixed with seed and fertilizer to use for patching lawns or establishing new flower beds. But to hydroseed anything larger than a few hundred square feet—really not much of a lawn—you'll probably save money by turning the work over to a landscaper.

SLICE SEEDING

Instead of hydroseeding, some landscapers spray out the existing vegetation, "scalp" mow to remove stubble and then sow grass seed just below the surface with a machine called a slice seeder. Bilodeau, however, has tested various techniques and finds that hydroseeding generally performs best, though sometimes he'll hydromulch instead. When he's using expensive wildflower seed mixes, for example, Bilodeau will sometimes slice seed an area to eliminate wasted seed, then he'll spray on seedless mulch. This is also the preferred method in arid climates, where the seed needs the extra protection that a soil layer provides (and where rototilling makes dry topsoil vulnerable to wind erosion).

A commercial seeding machine places seed beneath the soil. But a rake stiff enough to make grooves in the dirt works, too: The point is to provide a good contact between soil and seed.

overseeding

IF YOU THINK YOU NEED TO RIP OUT AN EXISTING, WEEDY LAWN IN ORDER TO GET REAL GREEN, THINK AGAIN. YOU CAN BEEF UP THIN, WEEDY TURF BY OVERSEEDING WITH NEW, PEST-RESISTANT GRASSES, AND THE BEST TIME TO DO IT IS EARLY FALL. BUT SPRING SOWING CAN WORK—IF STARTED EARLY. "THE LATER YOU GO, THE MORE WEEDS YOU'LL HAVE," SAYS MICHAEL TALBOT, WHO CARES ORGANICALLY FOR LAWNS IN THE BOSTON AREA. "YOU CAN CROWD THE WEEDS OUT OVER TIME, THOUGH."

FOR SMALL PATCHES, HE SCRATCHES UP THE SOIL WITH A RAKE, SCATTERS THE SEED AND TAMPS IT IN. THEN IT'S JUST A MATTER OF KEEPING THE SOIL MOIST UNTIL THE GRASS SPROUTS.

FOR LARGER AREAS, TALBOT MOWS THE LAWN SHORT, THEN SPREADS ANY SOIL AMENDMENT NECESSARY (IN HIS AREA, OFTEN ROCK PHOSPHATE AND GYPSUM). TO BREAK UP THE SURFACE, HE RUNS A POWER DE-THATCHER MOWER ACROSS THE LAWN. TOOL RENTAL YARDS CARRY THIS EQUIPMENT. "THEN RAKE UP ALL THE STUFF YOU'VE LOOSENED," TALBOT SAYS. HE SOWS SEEDS AT THE RATE RECOMMENDED FOR A NEW LAWN, OR A TOUCH MORE HEAVILY. TO GET SEEDS TO SETTLE, HE DRAGS THE LAWN WITH A RAKE, THEN GOES OVER THE AREA WITH A LAWN ROLLER, ALSO AVAILABLE AS A RENTAL.

TALBOT'S FINAL STEP IS TO TOP-DRESS THE AREA WITH A 1/4-INCH LAYER OF SCREENED COMPOST. HE BUYS ABOUT A CUBIC YARD TO TREAT 2,000 SQUARE FEET, BUT MATERIAL FROM A BACKYARD COMPOST PILE ALSO WORKS. "SCREEN IT THROUGH A 3/8- TO 1/2-INCH MESH," HE SUGGESTS.

[lawn edging]

MANNERS ALWAYS MATTER, but they're especially important on the frontier between two cultures. Even in that most peaceful of settings—the garden—territorial ambition can encroach on civil relations. Keeping peace between, say, the lawn and a bed of pansies isn't always easy. "Living plants grow," says Jim Brooks, of the Lawn Institute in Marietta, Georgia. "They move."

The lawn was invading the pansies (top) so Russ decided to separate the two. A sharp spade is essential for this work. To hone his spade, Russ strokes a mill bastard file against the back of the cutting edge, applying pressure only on the forward stroke. Then he leaps onto the spade (above), tips the spade back, then pulls it out. After he has loosened a few feet, he turns the spade 90 degrees and cuts the turf into chunks he can easily remove.

Which is why Russ Morash, the executive producer of *This Old House*, stepped into this green oasis with his garden hose, wheelbarrow and trusty flat-bladed, straight-edged garden spade. Instead of spading, some gardeners insist on using a physical edging barrier, of which there are many: brick, wood, stones, and neat edges of aluminum or steel. Russ, however, prefers the simplicity of a spade.

In subtropical Miami, where grass grows like a weed, Don Evans, director of horticulture at Fairchild Tropical Gardens, doesn't care much for "structural edges" either. But because Fairchild doesn't have them, his crew has to use gas-powered edgers to keep grass from sneaking up over miles of pathways and flower beds. Where looks are less crucial than ease of maintenance, concrete edging may be used. "Hard edging," Russ calls it, and with little sympathy. "You'd never use it in a proper garden. Too visually aggressive."

From this you get an idea of his taste about edging: clean, genteel, classical. His approach is called "cut edging." Russ describes it as "a classic English garden technique to define one area from another. In all the great gardens of England, this is what they'd do." And because it takes an edge to make an edge, he picks up a file and, with long, smooth strokes, sharpens his spade.

The grass in this garden, a mix of perennial rye and red fescue, has advanced much too close to the pansies. So Russ deploys his hose as a flexible cutting guide, stringing it out along the bed's new edge. Spading along this line will create a V-shaped trench like a moat, an eye-arresting curve.

When he started, Russ wasn't entirely happy with this pansy bed. He likes flower beds six or eight inches above grade; this one was only an inch or two up. But as he edged, he tossed the soil back among the flowers, knowing that eventually the bed would rise. He worked painstakingly, finishing perhaps a foot per minute. "Take your time and you'll get there faster," Russ's father used to say. In half an hour, he was packing up his tools.

[the problem lawn]

LEFT TO ITSELF, THE LAWN WOULD HAVE LOOKED LIKE MANY others—a variegated green studded with the gold of dandelions, spritzed with white clover and punctuated by those tall plantain things that the mower wouldn't cut. But Gary and Lynn McElfresh wanted a country-club lawn, an emerald carpet, and, like many families, they decided to let experts produce it. Like most such outfits, the lawn-care service fertilized and sprayed on a schedule. Like most home-owners, the McElfreshes didn't ask what chemicals the pros were using, assuming they knew what was safe.

watering *a lawn by hand is fine for newly seeded areas, but established lawns need deep irrigation. Grass roots run surprisngly deep.*

As recommended, the McElfreshes kept their cocker spaniel off the lawn for 12 hours after each spraying. But then Dasher began getting sick. The family vet said the dog's liver had failed and he would soon die. And then the vet mentioned an odd coincidence: She had seen six other dogs die for the same reason that year, and their owners had all used the same lawn-care service. There was no proof of cause and effect, but Gary suspected a link.

Many others are similarly concerned. Already ground-zero in a struggle with nature, the lawn has lately become the site of yet another turf war. One set of experts prescribes a course of chemicals guaranteed to produce a perfect carpet of grass; another group warns of health risks and environmental catastrophes associated with those chemicals. A home - owner feels bewildered, wondering how to grow a lawn that is both beautiful and environmentally friendly—green and green. Environmental experts are urging consumers to use restraint. "A typical home-owner applies more fertilizer and pesticide per acre than any farmer," says Marc Aveni, a cooperative extension agent in Prince William County, Virginia.

Evidence of environmental harm associated with lawn-care chemicals is slowly mounting, although some of it is conflicting. But it was the casualty in their own backyard that convinced the McElfreshes: They have gone organic. Technically, "organic" means any compound containing carbon, usually matter once alive. But for Clifford Maske, who now cares for the McElfreshes' lawn in

Bold stripes on a lawn (near right) indicate areas a fertilizer spreader failed to reach. Particularly with high-nitrogen synthetic fertilizers, uneven application can result in alternating bands of lush vegetation and burned leaves. In this case, it's also possible that the pH of the soil is not correct. A bull's-eye (far right) dead spot, especially when surrounded by lush grass, shows where a dog aimed. Urine kills the areas of grass it soaks, but its nitrogen fertilizes surrounding turf.

[the problem lawn]

Decatur, Illinois, "organic" applies to a philosophy of gardening he learned from his mother: chicken soup for the soil.

The basics of establishing a truly healthy lawn are the same for professionals and home-owners: planting grass varieties suitable for the area, testing the soil, adding organic material, mowing high, leaving clippings on the lawn to add nitrogen and organic matter to the soil, monitoring the lawn for pests, and spot-treating problems in as noninvasive a manner as possible. The process is slow. "It takes three years to regain soil health," Maske says. But proponents claim that maintenance is easier.

Fungal disease can kill patches of grass, but in this case the culprit is too much synthetic high-nitrogen fertilizer. A traditional approach would be to treat fertilizer burn with more careful application next time. Organic care greatly reduces the risk. Although raw manure can burn leaves, most commercial organic fertilizers are so low in soluble nitrogen that they do not.

UNDERSTANDING LAWN CARE

The first step: Assess whether to maintain the existing grass or switch it to some of the rugged new varieties with built-in resistance to drought, disease and pests. These include perennial ryegrasses ("Repell," "All Star," "Cowboy") and turf-type tall fescues ("Apache") bred with fungi called endophytes, which live between the grass cells and make the blades distasteful to leaf-eaters.

Maske decided that the McElfreshes—who moved after Dasher died to a house with a very rough lawn—needed to reseed with a mixture of endophytic grasses that stay green without much water. Weak, temperamental lawns can also be changed to the improved varieties by over-seeding. "It's usually worthwhile as long as turf grasses cover at least half the space," says Michael Talbot, an organic-lawn-care expert in Boston. If not, the lawn may need to be completely reestablished.

Professionals like Maske and Talbot have ready access to the improved varieties. For home-owners who can find only "grass mix" at their garden center, Talbot recommends looking for packages with diverse species and a notation on the label that at least some of the seed is "naturally insect-resistant"—code for endophytic. If no label says that or the only endophytic packages contain mostly ryegrass, a short-lived species, he recommends looking for a blend high in fine, tall *named* fescues—"anything in quotation marks," he says. This usually indicates a recent variety. A cooperative extension office, agricultural college, or organic lawn service can recommend the best types for a specific terrain.

For a nominal fee, the same experts can also test the soil. The sample should be mixed from several spots of the lawn. (Problem areas might warrant separate samples.) Most grasses thrive in slightly acidic to neutral earth, which has a pH of 6 to 7. Without the proper pH, the microorganisms that break down organic matter and release nutrients to plants are not as active. Adding ground limestone makes acidic soil more neutral; sulfur makes alkaline soil more acidic. People who don't test their soil may pour on too much lime or sulphur, or they may use the wrong kind of lime. "If the testing place recommends lime high in calcium, don't use dolomitic lime, which is high in magnesium," Talbot says. Correcting the pH also helps to discourage dandelions, which like slightly alkaline soil.

The soil test may also indicate that the grass needs nitrogen, phosphorus and potassium—those magic fertilizer ingredients represented by numbers like 10-5-5 on fertilizer bags.

What do the numbers mean? A 10-5-5 fertilizer is 10 percent nitrogen, 5 percent phosphorus and 5 percent potassium. To figure out the amount of nitrogen in a 25-pound bag, multiply the proportion (.1) by the weight of the bag; it contains 2.5 pounds of nitrogen. Typically, a 1,000-square-foot lawn on decent soil benefits from about a pound of nitrogen once or twice a year to stimulate roots during growth periods. For lawns planted with cool-season varieties—ryes, fescues, bluegrasses—the most important feeding is in early fall. Fertilizing in spring produces lush leaves but, if done too late or too liberally, it's at the expense of root development. These grasses should not be fertilized in summer because they are dormant then, especially if not irrigated. For lawns planted with warm-season varieties—Bermudas, saint augustine, centipede—the opposite applies. These grow in summer and benefit from late-spring fertilizing.

Man-made fertilizers often have a very high nitrogen content. Many consist of urea synthesized from ammonia and air; they can be more than 45 percent nitrogen. (A label doesn't always tell the whole story. Because synthetic urea also contains carbon dioxide, it can be called "organic.") The fertilizer produces lush blades, but the burst of growth depletes carbohydrate reserves needed for strong roots. Such synthetics are usually water-soluble, so much of the nitrogen leaches away with the first rain. This makes the fertilizer useless to the grass as well as a pollutant to nearby waterways. The compounds also burn grass if not carefully used. Some ureas are now polymer-coated for slower release.

Irregular areas of dead grass appear where beetle grubs have chewed off grass roots. Sometimes the damage shows up in spring when grubs resume feeding. But more severe damage usually occurs in early fall, from newly hatched grubs. Organic controls include parasitic nematores and formulations that spread milky-spore disease. The best defense is robust turf.

[the problem lawn]

ADDING ORGANIC MATERIAL

But no chemical fertilizer can add organic material. A chemically fertilized lawn, especially if the clippings are removed, eventually becomes virtually hydroponic, existing on only water and fertilizer. The lawn will need more additives to accomplish what the organisms do in healthy soil.

Most organic fertilizers do not dissolve in water. They are broken down slowly by the microorganisms. The kick these fertilizers provide is therefore not immediate, but it lasts longer. Organic fertilizers may be made from animal manures (poultry droppings are particularly high in nitrogen), sewage sludge (the best is dried activated sludge, made in a process using microorganisms), fish meal, blood meal, cottonseed meal or soybean meal. Good organic sources of phosphorus are bone meal and ground rocks containing calcium phosphate. Potassium, or potash, may come from wood ashes, greensand (a naturally occurring hydrated salt of iron and potassium silicate) or seaweed.

Because of their organic content, most natural fertilizers are bulkier than synthetics. They also cost more. But some organics are free: Clippings left where they fall supply significant amounts of nitrogen and potassium, reducing the need for fertilizer by half.

Composted yard waste can also help build the airy, loose soil that grass needs. A top dressing of 1/4 inch of fine compost breaks down thatch (the spongy layer of dead but not decomposed root runners that forms on over-fertilized, over-watered lawns). Recent studies show that some composts actually control diseases such as dollar spot, brown patch and red thread. If the thatch is thick or the soil dense and compacted, a core aerator may be needed to remove plugs of soil.

Cool-season grasses tend to brown during the summer if not irrigated. For green all season, aim for an inch of water a week. Watering early in the day reduces evaporation and the risk of disease. If the lawn isn't irrigated, it will resume growing when rain returns and become green again. But during the dormant period, more drought-resistant weeds may get a toehold.

A trail of footprints shows where someone crossed a frozen lawn, fracturing the brittle cell walls of the grass blades. With the first mowing in spring, the damage will disappear. Freezing temperatures can also cause scattered blades of grass to turn to straw. When the lawn resumes growing in spring, the dead leaves will disappear among all the fresh, new green.

OTHER LAWN STRATEGIES

"Even if you eat right," says Maske, "once in a while you have to take some medicine." The main organic weed-control medicine is corn gluten meal, the part of corn left after syrup is extracted. Spread early in the spring, corn gluten meal can keep weed seeds from sprouting. As the meal decomposes, it doubles as a fertilizer. Organic pest controls, available by mail order, include ladybugs, praying mantis, and cultures of specific bacteria and fungi. Talbot monitors lawns for grubs, sometimes rolling back sections of turf to find them. If he spots more than 10 grubs in a square foot, he introduces microscopic worms called nematodes, which arrive imbedded in a sponge. He soaks it in a bucket of water to release the nematodes, then sprays with the water. Where crows digging for grubs are the main problem, he spreads bird netting for a couple of weeks.

If all else fails, Talbot replaces problematic sections of lawn with ground cover or a pathway—and occasionally uses a spot application of an insecticide or herbicide. "People can eliminate 90 percent of their pesticide use by spraying just when and where it's needed," says Talbot. The McElfreshes did have a few dandelions in the first years of their organic lawn. But lush growth eventually choked out the weeds. Gary now scoffs at the "steroid shots" his old lawn needed. "Your lawn is not going to be green as quickly as one with chemicals, but over time it's even better," he says. "We'll compare our lawn to any other in the neighborhood."

the most *commonly used herbicide for home lawns is 2,4-D, a major component of the defoliant Agent Orange used in the Vietnam War.*

[lawn maintenance]

IN SPRING, WHEN LAWNS LOOK THEIR BEST, OUR OPTIMISM GROWS along with the burgeoning blades of grass. Surely, we hope, this plush carpet is there to stay. But as spring gives way to summer, drought and disease take their toll, and the emerald turf begins to show other colors—a paler green or, worse, yellow or brown. And that just won't do for anyone who wants an unblemished expanse of grass. The quest for perfection often leads to the application of massive and expensive doses of chemicals. But there are easier, less toxic ways to fix flaws *and* create a lawn that's virtually trouble-free.

in order to *burn 150 calories, you could push a powered lawnmower around the yard for about 29 minutes.*

Take weeds, for example. A few of them dotting the turf is little cause for concern, but when they threaten to dominate, think of the lawn as though it were a garden: Flower beds get weeded and so can lawns, and in a surprisingly short time with a long-handled tool that lets you stay on your feet. Once weeds have been eliminated, new ones can be stopped with an effective non-toxic herbicide: corn gluten meal. One application a year (about 10 pounds per 1,000 square feet, in early spring) can stop dandelions, crabgrass, purslane and other undesirables before they start. Spreading corn gluten in September will shut down such fall bloomers as henbit, chickweed, and crabgrass.

Eradicating weeds, however, only treats the symptom of a larger problem: poor soil and other conditions that inhibit turf growth and allow unwanted plants to elbow their way in. Nothing encourages weeds more than compacted soil. To find out if you have it, jam a screwdriver into the turf after a rainstorm; if sinking the shaft up to the handle takes a great deal of effort, the soil needs to be loosened up. For lawns under half an acre, a hand aerator—a couple of hollow tubes on a long handle—will do the job. When pushed into the lawn and then pulled out, the tubes extract sausages of soil and deposit them on the surface. For larger lawns, rent a power aerator. Follow the aeration with a top-dressing—covering the

« Nothing encourages weeds more than compacted soil. »

For This Old House host Steve Thomas, the pleasures of a plush lawn include getting out with an old-fashioned sprayer on a sunny day. Sprinkling by hand can help sprout newly planted seeds, but established lawns need deep irrigation.

[lawn maintenance]

lawn with a ¼-inch layer of sand, topsoil, or finely ground compost—which will help break up the soil even more and reintroduce beneficial microorganisms.

Some critters can kill large patches of grass. Grubs, for example, live underground as white-colored larvae that cut grass plants off at the roots. In cases of severe infestation, big mats of grass turn brown and become loose enough to lift from the soil. To check for these bugs, cut a square-foot patch of sod, roll it back, and look at the roots. If you find more than six or so grubs, treat the entire lawn in late summer or early fall with an insecticide containing carparyl or neem. Or apply milky spore, a safe bacterial agent that colonizes the soil and continues killing grubs year after year.

Other insects are usually minor nuisances, but occasionally chinch bugs, sod webworms, and billbugs, to name a few, do enough damage to warrant treatment. You'll see their handiwork as holes in individual blades and patches of dying turf. To look for blade-eating billbugs, run your hands over a square yard of grass; if more than 20 insects emerge, treat the lawn with insecticidal soap or pyrethrum. Crown-dwelling insects such as chinch bugs are more difficult to flush out because they spend most of their brief lives deep in the plant. To find them, remove both ends from a two-pound coffee can, sink it into the ground, and fill it with soapy water. If more than 10 insects land in the water after 15 to 30 minutes, the lawn ought to have a billbug treatment.

If it's not insects making your lawn look ratty, it could be a disease such as brown patch, dollar spot, fusarium patch, or snow mold. Any of these must be dealt with or they can turn grass into black mulch or create brown spots virtually overnight. If you look closely, you may see strands of fungus on the grass, and striped or rust-colored blades. Most diseases can be controlled by fungicides such as iprodione, thiram, and mancozep—at least temporarily. For the long run it's better to alter the conditions and practices that give rise to disease. These include too much shade, excessive moisture, poor air circulation and, ironically, too many applications of chemical herbicides, fungicides, pesticides, and fertilizer, all of which can kill worms, bacteria, and other beneficial soil life. Preventive measures include watering only when necessary (and never in the evening), fertilizing no more than twice a year, aerating the soil, and pruning shrubs and trees to reduce shade and improve air circulation. In some cases, the turf will have to be completely replaced with more disease-resistant or shade-tolerant variety. It may even be necessary to give up on grass entirely and put in ground covers or paving stones.

Lawn problems can also be caused by less sinister things than bugs or diseases: For instance, someone may have spilled gasoline, pesticide, or fertilizer; or the

Chinch bug. This critter devours grass blades.

Webworm. This one chews the crown of the plant.

White grub. Grubs gobble grass at the roots.

MOWING CAN BE THE BEST OR THE WORST THING YOU DO FOR YOUR LAWN. THE RIGHT TREATMENT INCLUDES CUTTING OFTEN—UP TO TWICE A WEEK—AND SETTING THE MOWER HIGH. HOW HIGH? EACH GRASS SPECIES HAS AN OPTIMUM HEIGHT: 4 INCHES FOR TALL FESCUE, 3 INCHES FOR BLUEGRASS AND SAINT AUGUSTINE GRASS, AND 2½ INCHES FOR RYEGRASS. HERE ARE SOME MORE TIPS:

REMOVING MORE THAN A THIRD OF THE BLADE SHOCKS THE PLANT, WHICH CAN WEAKEN THE TURF. IF A LAWN LOOKS A LITTLE BROWN THE DAY AFTER A MOWING, IT HAS BEEN CUT TOO LOW.

CUT THE GRASS SLIGHTLY BELOW ITS MAXIMUM HEIGHT THROUGH MOST OF THE SEASON, BUT RAISE THE MOWER ½ INCH DURING UNUSUALLY HOT OR DRY PERIODS.

IF THE LAWN TAKES ON A GRAY CAST AFTER MOWING, OR THE GRASS HAS RAGGED TIPS, THE MOWER BLADE SHOULD BE SHARPENED.

CUTTING ALONG THE SAME ROWS WEEK AFTER WEEK CAN CREATE RUTS OF COMPACTED SOIL. VARY YOUR ROUTE ABOUT ONCE A MONTH.

the right way to mow

[lawn maintenance]

neighborhood dog may have been making its rounds. Tree and shrub roots can also create bare spots, as can poor mowing practices. So to avoid over-treating a lawn, be sure to eliminate all these possibilities (and any others) before attacking bugs and diseases.

That's actually good advice for dealing with any problem—question the cause. Get to know your lawn. Find out where that shade lingers in the morning or where water puddles after a rain. Keep track of when you mow, water, and fertilize. In the process, you'll discover that lawn problems aren't such a mystery, and that solving them isn't difficult.

Trouble spots. **Here are some lawn problems to look for.** 1. Webworm. **Patches of dead grass with chewed-off blades are a sign that webworm larvae have been feeding. Some newer ryegrasses resist this insect.** 2. Fungus. **When grass suddenly turns brown, fungus is at work. Control it with a fungicide, then aerate and reduce shade to prevent its reoccurence.** 3. Weeds. **An invasion of weeds is a sign of soil compaction or poor drainage. After pulling them out, improve the soil to promote healthy turf.** 4. Thinning. **Thin turf may not be getting enough sun. Over-seed with a shade-tolerant variety grass.**

Bottom photos: ©judywhite/GardenPhotos.com

« To keep weeds, bugs, and diseases at bay, set the mower so it makes a high cut. »

[watering a lawn]

FOR MOST AMERICANS, A FRONT YARD MEANS an emerald moat of lush grass. Yet, without the humble lawn sprinkler or an underground sprinkler system (see page 12), houses might still be bordered by weeds and barrens of beaten dirt, as they were until the mid-19th century. The best watering strategy depends on more than oversimplified "rules" of thumb, however.

Old rule: Add 1 inch of water a week. Reality: Soils vary in their ability to absorb moisture. When damp to a depth of 9 inches, clay soil holds up to 3 inches of water, loam holds up to 2 inches and sandy soil holds less than an inch. The rate at which these soils absorb moisture runs in the opposite direction. Sandy soil takes in 1 inch of water an hour, clay just 1/10 inch. To test whether the ground is getting enough water, turn on a sprinkler for a set amount of time. Wait an hour; then use a shovel, hand trowel or soil probe to check moisture in the root zone. If soil is dry just a few inches down, turn the sprinkler back on and repeat the procedure. After learning what works best, set a timer. If water puddles off before soil is moistened sufficiently, get a timer with multiple cycles, which can switch on for 10 minutes, then off for an hour, then on again for 10 minutes.

The best way to see if a sprinkler is watering evenly? Set out rain gauges in several areas. If the gauges fill unevenly, try an overlapping sprinkler pattern, or a different sprinkler.

Old rule: Water only once a week. Reality: Instead of focusing on how many days since the last watering, learn to decipher the lawn's condition. If the blades are darker than normal, perhaps blue-gray, or if the grass doesn't spring back when walked on, water it.

When you water, water deeply. The best strategy is to dampen the entire root zone of the grass—but no more. Bent-grass roots reach down 1 to 8 inches. Dichondra, Kentucky bluegrass, red fescue, ryegrass and saint augustine grass have 8- to 18-inch roots. For Bermuda grass, crown vetch, tall fescue and zoysia, it's up to 5 feet. To check a lawn's roots, turn back a spadeful in an inconspicuous area and take a look; then push the sod back into place and water the area.

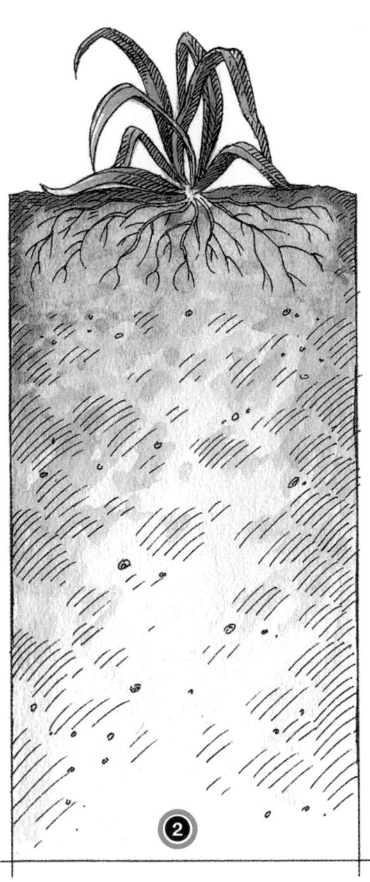

Old rule: Don't water in the heat of the day. Reality: A lawn so thirsty it turns dark might actually benefit from a brief watering immediately, regardless of time of day. Follow with a thorough irrigation at night or early the next day. It's true, though, that watering in the middle of the day is not good because too much water is lost to evaporation.

Old rule: Never water at night. Reality: The Cooperative Extension Service in Colorado recommends irrigating between midnight and 6 a.m., when the grass is already wet with dew but doesn't have long to wait for the drying rays of morning. This is practical only with a timer that turns the water on and off. The next best time to water is midday—after dew has dried but not so late that the grass won't dry by nightfall. The goal is to minimize evaporation losses while keeping the blades from being damp for more than 12 hours at a stretch, which encourages the growth of some fungal diseases.

Old rule: Lawn grasses go dormant in the summer, so it's OK not to have the lawn watered while you're vacation. Reality: Traditional turf grasses, such as Kentucky bluegrass, grow in cool weather and lie dormant in the summer if not watered. If irrigated regularly, they stay green. What they cannot do is adapt to on-again, off-again watering—especially if they have been over-fertilized, because rapid growth depletes their carbohydrate reserves. If a lawn must fall dormant, allow it do so gradually.

1. Thorough but infrequent watering promotes the growth of deep roots and robust leaves.

2. Waterlogged soil keeps roots from getting the oxygen they need, which reduces the growth of blades and roots.

3. Lack of moisture also stunts grass, reducing growth aboveground and below.

4. Light watering stimulates root growth only near the surface. When the ground dries out, the grass withers.

[fall lawn care]

LIKE KIDS WHO DON'T know how tired they really are, yards can't just go to sleep on their own—they have to be put to bed. The horticultural versions of warm milk and a good story vary from place to place, but the one sure thing is this: There's a lot more to maintaining lawns than just raking leaves.

fall
is a good time to over-seed thin areas. Lightly rough up the patches with a rake, sprinkle the seed, then keep it well-watered while it germinates.

Fall is the best time to nourish cool-season grasses such as Kentucky bluegrass and tall fescue. Dave Chalmers, turf specialist at Virginia Polytechnic Institute, recommends a fall fertility program for September, October and November. First, he says, test whether soil pH needs to be adjusted. A low pH (under 6) indicates acidic conditions, which will limit absorption of nutrients such as potassium and phosphate. Adding lime will raise the pH. "But it can take three to six months for lime to break down," says *This Old House* landscaping consultant Roger Cook, "so it makes sense to let that happen over winter."

To thicken grass and promote root development, soil with a balanced pH should still be fertilized with one pound of actual nitrogen per 1,000 square feet of lawn, divided into equal doses applied in September, October and November. Figure out how much actual nitrogen is in a bag by multiplying the labeled percentage by the package's total weight. "Ideally, the treatments should be four to six weeks apart," Chalmers says. "Farther north than the mid-Atlantic region, you can start earlier; farther south, a little later. If you want to cut back to two treatments, do them in October and November. If you only have time for one, go with October."

Many landscapers cut grass shorter as the season advances, down to 1¼ inches. Left long, turf invites snow mold and fungus diseases. Plus, with less dead grass in the way, the lawn will green up faster next spring.

fall care for warm-season grasses

IN THE SOUTH, SOUTHWEST AND TEMPERATE NORTHWEST, WARM-SEASON GRASSES SUCH AS BERMUDA, BAHIA, SAINT AUGUSTINE AND CENTIPEDE ARE COMMON. BECAUSE THERE IS LITTLE THREAT OF SNOW, LAWNS IN THESE AREAS CAN BE KEPT GREEN ALL WINTER BY SEEDING WITH A COOL-SEASON GRASS—SUCH AS ANNUAL RYEGRASS—SIX TO EIGHT WEEKS BEFORE THE FIRST HEAVY FROST, USING 10 POUNDS PER 1,000 SQUARE FEET OF LAWN. SOME SEED COMPANIES RECOMMEND FESCUE FOR WINTER GREENING. BEWARE: IT CAN SURVIVE INTO SUMMER AND CHOKE OUT WARM-SEASON GRASSES. IF YOU HAVEN'T PUT DOWN ANY SEED, APPLY A PRE-EMERGENT HERBICIDE SO BROADLEAF WEEDS WON'T RETURN WITH SPRING GROWTH. SPREAD LIME IF THE PH LEVELS FALL BELOW 5.5. FINALLY, DE-THATCH WHERE NECESSARY.

Autumn winds will blow off some lawn-bound leaves, but before the snows come, the rest have to go or they'll damage the turf. Wet and compacted, leaves feed grass-killing fungus and mold. A bag-equipped power mower can vacuum them away, but raking has benefits: breaking up thatch and stirring the surface of compacted soil. Beware of mowing too low. Scalping the grass, especially in early fall, removes too much of the upper blade, where the plant makes most of its food.

[the unlawn]

IT WAS A YARD UNLIKE others in the Phoenix suburb: the only one that wasn't flat and green. Instead, the gravelly soil was gently contoured, clumped with dry grasses among mats of bright desert flowers and crowned with mesquite and palo verde trees. Small yellow butterflies called sulphurs were nectaring at desert marigolds. The morning air, heating rapidly, lifted from the purple-flowered Texas ranger its startling scent: grape soda.

Xeriscape gardeners have many tricks for conserving water. Here, perennials were planted in hollow spots where rainwater collects.

The other yards were grass, watered in a way common in Phoenix: shaped into a shallow basin and flooded by a gusher. Fifty percent of the water used by households here is squandered on landscape. Yet the only oasis in this green-carpeted subdivision was the one dry yard. That a grassy yard is lifeless compared with a gritty one may surprise those who lavish attention on lawns. But Phoenix is desert, and landscape designer Carrie Nimmer simply followed nature. What maintenance chores are required of such a yard? "Weeding," notes Nimmer, pointing ruefully to a tuft of grass that had crept in from the neighbor's lawn.

In recent years, a move toward natural gardens has been gaining ground across the country. Home-owners are restoring natural vegetation not only because they like watching butterflies, but also because a landscape that supports wildlife rarely requires pesticides, fertilizers or water.

XERISCAPING

Phoenix lies in the northeast corner of the Sonoran desert, where annual precipitation averages 7½ inches and summer temperatures often climb past 110 degrees. Desert vegetation is adapted to this harsh climate. Some plants have leaves that are heat-reflecting gray or are waxy, thick and leathery. Other plants have no leaves, including the cacti, whose green and water-hoarding stems make food by photosynthesis. Many dryland flowers spend the greater part of their lives as seeds, lying patiently in the desert grit, awaiting the wash of rain that signals them to sprout, bloom and then to harden new seed against the inevitable return of drought. To botanists, plants that have evolved such strategies against desiccation are known as xerophytes—"dry plants."

By definition, deserts have less than 10 inches of rain a year. But there are other xeric environments as well. Summer drought dries

Nimmer installed a simple drip irrigation system with individual emitters to keep one arid-climate garden growing. Here, an Angelita daisy gets water only when it needs a drink.

[the unlawn]

in a natural *ecosystem, pests are controlled by predators and by the physical and chemical defenses of the plants.*

up Western yards, wind sucks moisture from Nebraska lawns, and water runs right through the sandy gardens of the Atlantic shore. Like desert vegetation, the natural communities of plants that occur in these environments require little water. And a yard planted with such unthirsty species has come to be called a Xeriscape.

Xeriscaping is a water-conserving design strategy devised by the Denver Water Conservation Department during a 1970s drought. In Xeriscape gardens, the land is contoured to direct and contain rainfall, and gravel or another mulch is used to cut down on evaporation. Plants are chosen for their ability to withstand drought. Many Arizona Xeriscapes, including Nimmer's, get a boost from buried drip irrigation lines. Without supplemental water in unusually dry years, Nimmer says, even well-adapted Sonoran perennials may die and desert annuals may fail to germinate. Drip irrigation also allows gardeners to cultivate a wider range of plants and promotes faster growth.

Nimmer's creation includes a flow of smooth river cobbles to simulate a wash. Though contrived to please the eye, the dry stream also conserves water: Stones that are fist-size or broader cut down on surface evaporation. Nimmer uses large rocks, too, to create microhabitats. Perennials installed at their east-facing bases receive good morning light but are protected from brutal heat later in the day.

Natural ecosystems are self-sufficient. The nutrients in plant litter are recycled through animal and microbial digestive systems. Soil is turned, aerated, made porous and water-absorbing by burrowers of every size, from ants to gophers. Flowers are pollinated by birds, bats and insects; their seeds are dispersed by animals as well. Pests are controlled by predators and by the physical and chemical defenses of the plants. Everything is synchronized: The system runs itself and costs nothing.

FROM LAWN TO MEADOW

To some, lawns are sterile second cousins to Astroturf. By contrast, a meadow buzzes with birds and insects and swirls with a rich variety

1. This landscaping is typical of many neighborhoods: a broad expanse of Bermuda grass with little to distinguish it.

2. Soon after it was redone, the yard looked sparse, but elements were in place for a landscape more suited to the desert. A flagstone path coursed past grasses, succulents, and a mesquite tree; an irrigation system hid beneath pebble mulch.

3. One year after planting, Regal Mist grass put on a fall show of smoky maroon. Across the path bloomed licorice marigold and orange jubilee.

[the unlawn]

of plant life. Natural fields need no chemicals—their innate diversity resists pests—and they never require raking or watering. "If there were an Eden," says Jeffrey Glassberg, of the North American Butterfly Association, "it would be a meadow."

Why are meadows so fecund? The answer lies underground, with the roots. Cool-season grasses, the kind covering most lawns, have roots that spread in a thick fibrous mat, squeezing out most other plants. Meadow grasses, by nature, are less authoritarian. In the Northeast, for instance, the native grasses such as little bluestem grow in compact clumps, leaving space for a colorful profusion of wildflowers. The caterpillars that thrive on the flowers' leaves become the butterflies that soak up the blossoms' nectar. Birds dine on a smorgasbord of insects and seeds. Meadows," says Glassberg, "are ecological picnics."

Although slower than their high-powered relatives, quiet hand tools have a natural place in the making of a field. Here, a sharpened grub hoe is being used to root out a tenacious gray-stemmed dogwood stump.

You don't need much space for a meadow; a 10-by-10-foot corner of a suburban yard that receives at least four hours of sun a day will do just fine. Unlike the natural grasslands of prairies or mountains, meadows in the Northeast are ephemeral. They appear suddenly whenever fire or windstorms clear an opening big enough for the grasses and wildflowers to take hold, and then slowly disappear as the forest reclaims its turf.

It's not enough just to clear the scrub in an old field or to sprinkle a can of wildflower seeds over a lawn. Landscape designer Larry Weaner, a noted authority on meadows, says, "You need to literally root out the woody plants or they'll grow right back up." And if you have a lawn, the grass has to go, too. "It will smother everything," says Weaner. He recommends killing it with a short-lived, broad-spectrum herbicide, and leaving the grasses' dead roots to nourish the soil.

When faced with a phalanx of scrub, meadow-makers haul out the heavy armor—brush mowers, chainsaws and rotary trimmers. Once cut, the field can be double-tilled with a cultivator (although Weaner warns this encourages weeds) or it can be covered with rolls of black plastic. The heat buildup underneath kills just about everything in a few weeks—no herbicides required.

Weaner rakes the cleared area, then sows it with native grass seed, available through catalogs. In his view, planting only wildflowers is a bad idea. "The mixture should have at least 40 percent grass to hold off the weeds," he says. "Otherwise it will end up looking like an untended garden."

Maintaining a meadow is blissfully simple: Simply cut it once a year with the brush mower set at about 6 inches high. This is a project for very early spring, which allows the birds to feast on the seeds all winter and nest undisturbed through the summer.

A field springs to life with ever-changing hues—from the lavender of thistle to the starry white of the wood aster. Even in the snow, stalks of bluestem point skyward, a golden promise of the spring to come.

Around this house in Churchtown, New York, the scrubby overgrowth that had invaded an old cow pasture has been hacked down and turned into a meadow filled with native grasses and flowers. It is a scene that appears perfectly natural, despite the effort that went into making it.

[planting trees]

EVER SINCE NORM built his dream house a few years ago, the yard has been a work-in-progress. Fall is an excellent time for planting, so that's when Norm and *This Old House* landscape consultant Roger Cook put in a towering sugar maple along the side patio, replacing another one that didn't make it because of a bad root system. The arboreal duo also added a dwarf cypress, one of Norm's favorites, as well as two Japanese maples in front, to create a privacy barrier. "They really make the driveway disappear," says Norm. "And I love the look of those weeping trees, expecially in the fall when they turn a fiery red." To create room for growing herbs, Roger and Norm removed some perennials near the house. Free-form beds surrounding the trees add visual interest to the yard and make the house look more "settled," says Norm. "The best part, though, is that I have less grass to cut."

TO CHOOSE A TREE, FIRST VISIT A FULL-GROWN SPECIMEN. FEW NURSERIES CARRY LONG-LIVED NATIVE TREES, CONCENTRATING INSTEAD ON THE MORE POPULAR DECORATIVE TREES. THE NATIONAL ARBOR DAY FOUNDATION CAN SUPPLY THE NAME OF THE CLOSEST SOURCE FOR THE TREE YOU CHOOSE. PURCHASE THE LARGEST TREE YOU CAN AFFORD (GO BY TRUNK SIZE, NOT JUST HEIGHT). BRANCHES SHOULD BE WELL-SPACED, FORMING "Ls" (A 45° ANGLE TO THE TRUNK) NOT "Vs". THE SOIL AROUND THE ROOT BALL SHOULD BE FIRM BUT FRIABLE, NOT CLAYLIKE OR HARD.

shopping for a tree

Roger Cook (left) waters as Norm spreads mulch around a new sugar maple at his house.

TECHNIQUES

Standard tree-planting routines—dig a hole, plant the tree, fill with dirt, water—assume near-perfect conditions. Adverse conditions, such as those in south Florida, where soil is only a foot deep, call for different strategies.

1 Hand-digging is possible, but the work goes more quickly with a truck-mounted drill rig. The 42-inch bit dredges up a furrow of material. Remove large rocks and any debris that may interfere with root growth.

2 Get a good grip on the trunk and support the root ball, then haul the tree toward the hole. This tree is an 8-foot container-grown mahogany (*Swietenia mahagoni*). Larger trees require two people for transport.

3 Cut the container away and loosen the roots. (Don't pull the tree out or the crown—where the trunk meets the roots—may be damaged.)

4 The local potting soil is equal parts Everglades muck, peat moss, and sand; fertilizer tablets may be added. In other parts of the country, however, a tree might be backfilled with a mixture of soil and leaf mulch.

TECHNIQUES

5 Put a foot of the potting mix in the hole, then fill the hole with water and let it drain.

6 Put the tree in the hole, center it, and then fill the hole halfway with the planting mix. Add 2 tablespoons of Terra Sorb, a water-storing polymer, and 5 tablets of slow-release fertilizer. Then water thoroughly.

7 Now straighten the tree, using a level to get it into the ballpark and your eyeballs to fine-tune it. Step back and scrutinize the angle, then walk around the tree to view it from other vantage points. Bring the soil up to the crown, checking with a board placed across the hole.

Water is the key to a good start. When the tree is in place, make a berm of soil around the circumference of the planting hole to act as a catch basin. Water deep and often for the first season. Once established, a properly planted native tree will care for itself.

[pruning]

YOUR YARD IS A JUNGLE. YOUR shears are sharp. But before hacking a path to Dr. Livingston, lie down for a quiet moment under the trunk of a young tree. Stare skyward. Imagine a beach umbrella. "You should be able to see through the branches but still have an umbrella-like canopy," says Dennis Ryan. This is advice that comes from someone who looks at trees the way others look at fine paintings.

crossed *branches damage each other. Prune out one or the other as soon as a "sore spot" appears, if not before.*

Ryan, a professor of arboriculture and urban forestry at the University of Massachusetts, says visualization is the key to pruning trees and shrubs effectively. "Use your artistic eye," he says. "Try to visualize the tree 10 or 15 years down the road. Will the branches crowd each other out when they're larger?" Like ribs in an umbrella, uncrowded branches support a full leafy canopy and improve a tree's ability to make food through photosynthesis. Pruning shrubs requires a similar leap of imagination; most varieties of shrubs develop dense interiors that should be opened to more light. "The idea is to encourage the strong branches. Work from the inside, not the outside."

Ultimately, the pruner aims to promote healthy growth patterns. "If you don't prune, Mother Nature will," says Ryan. Allowing weak branches to survive invites breaking and tearing, especially during high winds and heavy snows. But trimming too much can be equally problematic. "Never remove more than 25 percent of the live wood," says Ryan, "because, along with the branches, you're also removing leaves, the plant's food factories."

The art of balanced tree pruning begins with developing strong scaffold branches, the major limbs that extend from the trunk. "Look at the branches of a young tree," says Ryan. "The ones you want to keep are attached to the trunk at a wide angle, the way your thumb is attached to your hand. The ones to prune are those which originate at sharp V-shaped crotches." The tight angle creates a weak spot at the crotch, making it more likely to be torn off under stress.

Branches that intersect are troublesome, too. "The danger comes when crossed branches rub against one another and cause an uncallused wound," writes gardening expert and author Robert Kourik. "There is a chance that the open lesion can be an entry point for pests and diseases."

Sometimes a tree has two trunks, called leaders, each vying for predominance. With some species, neither will ever have enough strength, and the rivalry should be ended by removing one of the leaders when the tree is very young. But lopping off the upper portion of the trunk of a mature tree can be disastrous.

Prime time for pruning. The ideal season for pruning varies according to the plant. Evergreen shrubs such as yew and juniper should be pruned at the first hint of spring. Likewise, for shrubs vulnerable to frost, such as rhododendron and azalea, Ryan recommends pruning out dieback—withered branches that won't support new growth—after the snow melts and the ground has started to thaw: "This will assure that water will be available as the shrubs put out new growth." Live branches of spring-flowering trees and shrubs should be pruned right after flowering. "Dogwood, flowering cherry, crab apple, rhododendron, azalea and forsythia are ideally pruned immediately after their flowers have withered and dropped off," says Ryan. "Prune too early, and you cut off this year's buds; wait too long, and you'll remove the following spring's buds." Whenever you prune, however, don't cut too close to the base of the branch

[pruning]

Known as topping, this crude approach is usually a last-ditch means of shortening a tree that has grown so tall that it blocks a cherished view or interferes with utility wires. A topped tree spreads out along its upper reaches in a flat, wide growth pattern and, says Kourik, will likely "die much sooner due to rot and disease entering the exposed leaders, limbs and branches." The best way to avoid the eventual need for topping is to thin lateral branches selectively.

As with trees, the art of pruning shrubs depends on foresight. "The first rule with shrubs is to make sure they're planted in the right place so they won't present a problem as they grow taller," says Ryan. "If you have to lower a shrub, cut the main stems down to lateral branches at the desired height." Called drop-crotch pruning, this technique changes the shape of a shrub by directing new growth outward rather than upward. By contrast, when outward growth is the problem—the

Before. **To give this lilac a better shape and improve its flowering potential, landscape contractor Walt Jamroga reduces its height and cuts out useless suckers and dead branches. When branches cross and rub against one another, sometimes creating open wounds, Jamroga lops off the branch that is weaker or growing toward the center of the shrub.**

After. **The finished job shows how pruning opens up the inside of a shrub to more light by selectively removing live inner branches. To the novice, a properly pruned shrub may look scraggly and bare at first; that may be one reason why shrubs (and trees) are often pruned too lightly. But new growth will demonstrate how useful a good pruning can be.**

shrub presses against the house or crowds other shrubs—trim the laterals. When branches grow longer on one side of a shrub than on the other, usually because of uneven exposure to sunlight, the solution is counterintuitive. In springtime, prune the long side lightly and the short side heavily, Kourik advises. The reason: Trimming the shorter branches prompts them to grow faster.

With trees or shrubs, cutting in the right place is critical. Alex Shigo, a tree biologist, teacher, and author of *100 Tree Myths*, pioneered one of the most important pruning innovations, the abandonment of the flush cut. "Years ago, we removed branches as close as possible to the bough," says Shigo. "Today's practice is to avoid cutting into the collar at the base of the branch." The collar, a raised shoulder of bark and wood, protects the wound within the first year after pruning. It's also a mistake to cut too far out from the collar, because a stub invites microorganisms to enter the plant.

The bark of a tree or shrub is similar to human skin, and piercing it makes the entire organism vulnerable. The secret of good pruning is not to hack like a jungle explorer but to visualize a healthy growth pattern, then wield the shears with a surgeon's care.

Before. **When his 10-year-old stewartia turns 20, Walt Jamroga wants it to be neither too wide nor too high for the garage it fronts and the shrubs it stands near.**

After. **To promote the shape and look he wants, Jamroga removes some interior branches and others that are too horizontal. Next year, he'll study the new growth and prune away any that don't fit into his plan.**

« The first rule with shrubs is to make sure they're planted in the right place so they won't present a problem as they grow taller," says Ryan. »

[moving trees]

RUSS MORASH TREASURED his dwarf evergreens but didn't like his yard's overall design. So he remodeled the landscape one spring, reusing many of his shrubs and small trees. He dug deep and wide—to get generous root balls—but suggests a more foolproof method would be to begin a year ahead. "Go out about a foot from the trunk with a spade and cut down about a foot deep all around the tree. It's what they do in nurseries." Then, on moving day, few of the large roots will need to be severed. Two adults can move trees with 3-inch trunks and root balls 2½ feet across. Extra help, however, never hurts.

A sharp spade is the tool of choice for releasing a shrub or tree from its home plot (below). Before you get started, however, gather the materials you'll need to protect the root ball, including burlap and twine. After lifting the root ball clear of the hole, Russ wraps it up, quick as a cowpoke roping a calf.

Don't lift by the trunk; wrap roots in burlap and grab onto that or a rope binding to scoot or "walk" the plant along. After sliding his bushes to a holding area, Russ shoveled on wood chips to keep the roots cool and moist until he could replant, taking care then to set trunks no deeper than before. Home-owners can skip the mycorrhizal fungi and rooting hormone used by professional tree transplanters. Inoculation requires special gear, and the fungi are usually present in established gardens anyway. "And even without rooting hormone," says Gary Watson of the Morton Arboretum, "you get up to a dozen little roots being produced from every cut root, probably in excess of what the tree needs."

When a tree is safely in its new home, don't plant anything on top of the root ball or even walk across it. "That's like beating up someone after he's had a heart transplant," says Texas tree-grower Tom Cox.

Moving a big tree, such as the Japanese maple at right, is a job for pros. Jim Ingram, of the F.A. Bartlett Tree Expert Co., says that in New England alone the company moves four or five huge trees each year, plus dozens more with trunks 10 to 12 inches across. Most cost just hundreds, not thousands, of dollars to hoist from one spot in a yard to another.

[removing trees]

PEOPLE LOVE TREES. But as long as they continue to build their houses near them, the trees will have to be pruned and, occasionally, cut down. Taking a tree down is the arborist's last resort, done only when the tree is standing dead, clearly dying, or sure to cause problems in the future. Near the house or not, a dead or dying tree should be taken down as soon as possible. Waiting might allow so much rot to take hold that a tree company will refuse to put a climber in it. A tree that is unhealthy or leaning over a house poses a threat, but a good arborist may be able to save it by selectively pruning new growth in the crown, cutting out deadwood, cabling leaders and split trunks together, and taking off big limbs.

But there is no greater scorn than that which reputable tree companies reserve for fly-by-night outfits. In the old days, jacklegs—as these operations were called—would go door-to-door with a truck and chain saw, offering their services but working with little regard for a tree's health or the home-owner's interests.

Like most contractors, tree companies vary in the quality of their work, and the one offering the lowest price isn't necessarily the one to choose. Bad pruning can kill a marginal tree, and then it it will cost more money to take down. Make sure that the company has insurance for personal injury, property damage and workmen's compensation. Be skeptical of tree workers who look for jobs by canvassing a neighborhood. Most good companies get all the work they need via advertising and referrals. And if a tree needs pruning, ask how it will be climbed. Workers should never wear spikes, because they leave the bark with unsightly tears that can also become entry points for viruses. To save money, you may get a tree company to take the tree down, leaving you to handle the clean-up and wood removal. Just make sure the arrangement is clearly spelled out in a contract.

who owns that tree?

FOR THE MOST PART, **LAWS REGARDING TREES ARE UNAMBIGUOUS. FOR INSTANCE, IF THE COMPLETE TRUNK OF A TREE STANDS ON YOUR PROPERTY, THE TREE BELONGS TO YOU; IF SOME PORTION OF ITS BOUGHS AND ROOTS REACH INTO YOUR NEIGHBOR'S LOT, SHE HAS THE RIGHT TO TRIM THEM—UP TO THE PROPERTY LINE ONLY. BUT SHE WOULD BE WISE TO ENGAGE A PROFESSIONAL TREE SERVICE, BECAUSE INJURING A TREE CAN BE A LIABLE OFFENSE. AND THE TREE-OWNER MUST GIVE PERMISSION IF, IN ORDER TO PERFORM THE WORK, THE ARBORIST MUST USE A LADDER, CLIMB THE TREE, OR GO ONTO THE OWNER'S PROPERTY. WHEN A TREE TRUNK STRADDLES A PROPERTY LINE, IT IS A "BOUNDARY TREE" AND BELONGS TO BOTH OF THE NEIGHBORS.**

Call a tree company immediately if a tree shows any of these signs:

- Large branches that are dead or broken and hanging.
- Cavities or mushrooms at the base of the trunk, noticeable amounts of rotten wood, or patches of missing bark.
- Cracks or seams where major limbs attach.
- Other dead trees in the immediate area, particularly after nearby excavation work.
- A trunk that has much more of a lean than that of surrounding trees.
- Roots or trunk damaged by heavy equipment, construction, or soil addition or removal.
- Signs of extreme pruning such as topping (removing most of the crown), which can weaken and kill a tree.

AFTER a day and a half, THE TILE WAS FINISHED AND THE GRILL WAS DROPPED IN. FINALLY: A perfect place to COOK and entertain.

[outdoor lights]

LOW-VOLTAGE GARDEN LIGHTING IS CHEAP, EASY TO INSTALL, and best of all, it eliminates the two big drawbacks of working with high-voltage lighting: restrictive local electrical codes and the risk of shock. The essential item here is the step-down transformer, which alters a home's 120-volt alternating current (AC) to 12-volt direct current (DC). Low-voltage DC is too weak to kill or even seriously hurt you—which is why it's used for children's train sets and small household appliances. But it's strong enough to light your garden, as long as you pay attention to the bulbs you use and the size and length of the connecting cable. Here are the parts of a typical system:

Fiber-optic lighting offers an alternative to 12-volt systems, though it is expensive and not as widely available. In such systems, the light from a single bulb speeds through slender plastic strands to each light fixture. Fixtures are best as spots; they won't light a wide area.

Transformers range from 25 to 600 watts in ouput. To choose one, add the wattage of all the lights you'll need. The transformer wattage should be about 20 percent higher than this number.

Outlets outdoors must be weatherproofed and have GFCI (ground-fault circuit interrupter) features. Never use extension cords, even with GFCIs, between an outlet and the transformer.

Connectors are simple plastic slides with metal teeth. Clamped shut on cable, the metal teeth penetrate the insulation to tap current.

Cable (wire) is measured by gauge: 10, 12, 14, 16 and 18. The lower the number, the thicker the cable, and the more current it carries. Use landscape-lighting cable: It's not affected by sunlight (which makes regular cable brittle) and its insulation is self-sealing, so if you move a fixture, connector holes will close up without needing special attention.

The best outdoor lighting plan emphasizes the effects, not the fixtures; fixtures should be unobtrusive. When lighting a walkway, place fixtures so they don't shine into a person's eyes. To do otherwise is discourteous and unsafe.

[outdoor lights]

Fixtures should be made of sturdy, rustless materials, such as thermoplastic, cast aluminum, ceramic or copper. These will also survive the occasional swat from a garden tool.

Bulbs typically rate from 7.5 to 75 watts, use less electricity than household bulbs and are smaller and

longer-lasting. Glass-base bulbs won't corrode as readily as metal bases do.

Before you can install a system, design a lighting plan. Make a scale drawing of your property and decide where you want the lights to go. Then trail a clothesline from the transformer to every proposed light site, marking each change in direction with rot-proof stakes. Use straight runs where possible, avoiding planting beds and borders that will be rototilled. Measure the clothesline to figure out how much cable to buy. Then, with the transformer unplugged, attach the cable according to manufacturer's instructions. Run the cable—above ground—along the staked route. Attach the fixtures, add bulbs, wait until nightfall and then plug in the transformer. Adjust the lights until you're happy with the results.

To bury the cable, use an edger or a straight-bladed spade, and cut through the turf at a 45-degree angle. Low-voltage wires should be 12 inches below ground, or as required by your local building codes. Pry up the lip of turf and push the cable all the way in. For extra safety, bury yellow plastic construction ribbon with the cable to alert diggers (cut wires won't injure them, but cable splices will be required). Don't cut off excess cable—you may want to add a couple of fixtures later. Just seal the end with electrical tape, and bury it. Drive the marking stakes to ground level so you can locate the cable later.

Mount the transformer (left) at least one foot above ground somewhere on the house, to make late-night adjustments easier. This granite fixture (right) is lit by a small candle, but similar fixtures can be fitted with 12-volt lighting.

getting the light right

ACCOMMODATING VOLTAGE DROP: BECAUSE OF CABLE'S INHERENT RESISTANCE TO THE FLOW OF ELECTRICITY, VOLTAGE DROPS ALONG A CABLE'S LENGTH, SO END-OF-RUN LAMPS WILL BE DIMMER THAN THOSE AT THE BEGINNING. SOME DROP IS INEVITABLE, BUT TRY TO LIMIT IT TO LESS THAN 2 VOLTS OUT OF THE 12.

VOLTAGE DROP IS CALCULATED BY MULTIPLYING THE TOTAL NOMINAL WATTAGE (TNW), OR ALL YOUR LIGHTS COMBINED, BY FEET OF CABLE AND DIVIDING BY A CABLE-RESISTANCE CONSTANT.

CABLE-RESISTANCE CONSTANT VALUES

GAUGE	18	16	14	12	10
CONSTANT	1,380	2,200	3,500	7,500	11,920

EXAMPLE: YOU HAVE SIX 27-WATT LAMPS AND A RUN OF 120 FEET. WITH 12-GAUGE CABLE (CONSTANT 7,500), YOUR VOLTAGE DROP WILL BE GREATER THAN 2 VOLTS; THAT'S TOO MUCH:

6x27=162 162x120=19440 19440/7500=2.592

YOU CAN REDUCE VOLTAGE DROP BY USING LOWER-WATTAGE LAMPS FOR SMALLER TNW; USING A HEAVIER GAUGE OF CABLE; OR MOVING THE TRANSFORMER TO A CENTRAL POSITION, DIVIDING THE CABLE INTO TWO 60-FOOT RUNS OF THREE LAMPS EACH.

lighting design basics

TOM WIRTH, LANDSCAPE ARCHITECT FOR THIS OLD HOUSE, SAYS, "MOST MISTAKES INVOLVE OVER-LIGHTING. THE PHOTOS IN MANUFACTURERS' BROCHURES CAN MAKE A HOUSE RESEMBLE A PENAL COLONY." HERE ARE SOME ADDITIONAL GUIDELINES FOR SUCCESSFUL OUTDOOR LIGHTING PROJECTS:

1. DON'T INSTALL THE SAME LIGHTS EVERYWHERE. VARY THE BREADTH, DEPTH (OR "THROW") AND INTENSITY OF BULBS. A VERY NARROW SPOT CAN THROW A FOCUSED BEAM ABOUT 30 FEET; A VERY WIDE FLOOD FANS SOFT LIGHT INTO A CONE UP TO 40 FEET WIDE.

2. SELECT THE RIGHT FIXTURE FOR FUNCTION AND APPEARANCE. ON A STAIRWAY, FOR EXAMPLE, USE SMALL LIGHTS TO EVENLY ILLUMINATE EACH STEP, RATHER THAN A LARGE GLOBE THAT CASTS TRICKY SHADOWS. DON'T EMPHASIZE THE FIXTURES OVER THEIR EFFECT. THEY SHOULD BE UNOBTRUSIVE, NIGHT AND DAY.

3. DON'T TRY TO TURN NIGHT INTO DAY. IF YOU OVERLIGHT, EVEN FOR SAFETY, YOU CAN CREATE "HOT SPOTS" OF HARSH LIGHT. MIX SUBTLE "EFFECT" LIGHTING ON HOUSE AND GROUNDS, WITH SAFETY LIGHTS AT ENTRANCES, PATHS, STAIRS OR GRADE CHANGES.

4. IF YOU OVERLIGHT THE LANDSCAPE, A HOUSE LEFT IN DARKNESS CAN TAKE ON A SINISTER, CHARLES ADDAMS LOOK. THIS IS UNSAFE AS WELL AS UN-APPEALING.

5. DON'T INSTALL SO MANY LIGHTS ALONG A WALKWAY THAT IT RESEMBLES AN AIRPORT RUNWAY. EXCEPT FOR VERY LONG PATHS, ONE FIXTURE AT THE FRONT AND ONE AT THE SIDEWALK SHOULD BE ENOUGH. FOR LIGHT IN BETWEEN, EXPERIMENT WITH "MOON-LIGHTING" FIXTURES MOUNTED HIGH IN TREES.

6. BE A GOOD NEIGHBOR. DON'T SHINE LIGHTS DIRECTLY ONTO AN ADJACENT HOUSE.

7. UNLIKE 110-VOLT CABLE, WHICH MUST BE SHEATHED AND DEEPLY BURIED FOR SAFETY, 12-VOLT CABLE CAN BE SLID INTO A SLIT MADE BY A SHOVEL (LEFT).

[building cold frames]

VISITORS TO RUSS MORASH'S GARDEN GAWK AT HIS BROWN-EYED Susans, larger than any they've seen. They lust after his delicate European lettuces and his heirloom cherry tomatoes. Everything, from radishes to rhododendrons, is stellar. One reason is that he nurtures his plants—but not too much. He starts them in his greenhouse or in pots parked on windowsills.

When they've grown a bit, he moves them out of these cozy spots to a row of clear-topped wooden boxes—his cold frames—beside his vegetable garden. They provide some shelter, but raising seedlings is not unlike raising children: The goal is to wean young ones from being pampered so they are hardy enough to survive life outside. "You don't want them to grow too quickly," he says of his plants. "You want them to get accustomed to hardship."

Russ's cold frames go into use in early spring as nurseries for tender plants, evolve into summertime halfway houses for cuttings that need special care, and wind up as permanent homes for his final crops of the year. Some northern gardeners harvest salad greens from cold frames all winter, but Russ, the executive producer of *This Old House*, picks his last lettuces late in the fall.

Even when nights are below freezing, afternoon sunshine can quickly bake plants inside a cold frame. For gardeners with time to putter, it's a pleasant daily ritual to raise the lid when the sun shines. Busier gardeners will want a solar-powered vent that automatically opens the lid when the inside gets too hot. During the summer, the tops should be removed and replaced with shade cloth or lath to shelter plants from too much sun.

Russ's first cold frames had old storm windows for lids. "But there comes that windy March day when everything falls apart and you have to pick the shards of glass out of the seedlings," he says. It's not much fun." He tried using corrugated plastic for lids but much prefers double-wall polycarbonate, the material used in many modern greenhouses. The plastic sheets have channels that create an insulating layer of air. The top edge is sealed with foil tape to keep out rain; the bottom edge is covered with a breathable white fabric tape that allows any moisture inside to escape. The plastic sheets are lightweight and sturdy. "We've never replaced a piece yet," Russ says.

A cold frame comes together: Norm Abram devised this cold frame. 1. Using a circular saw, Norm ripped both side pieces at an angle, from full width in back to 8 inches in front. Then he cut a 5-degree bevel on the front and back pieces. The resulting slopes will drain water nicely. 2. Front and back pieces were secured to the sides with $3^1/_2$-inch galvanized deck screws. 3. The cover frame was made from 2x6s ripped in half and half-lapped for strength at the corners. Norm routed a groove for the glazing, then screwed on narrow wood strips to hold glazing in place. 4. Hinges hold the top to the frame.

It's possible to buy a cold frame, but making one is a satisfying project. Russ's frame (below) is simply a floorless box with a lid. Norm's frame (facing page) is sized to suit plastic nursery trays and has a sloped top to drain rain. The side pieces are 39 inches long, and the front and back pieces are 51 inches long. Use an outdoor wood, but choose preservative-treated lumber with care (see page 130) to prevent chemicals that could affect plants from leaching out of the wood.

[playing safely]

YOU MIGHT THINK that grass is the ideal setting for a backyard playset, but no matter how good it looks, it isn't suitable beneath a backyard play structure. There should be a cushion wherever a head can hit, and grass is too hard—especially after the kids have compacted it into pavement. Grass is tough to maintain, too. Mowing around the post accessories of a typical swingset is like threading a needle with mittens on.

Covering the play area with 2-inch-thick rubber mats (above), common in public playgrounds, will probably cost more than the playset itself.

At public playgrounds, the U.S. Consumer Product Safety Commission recommends a cushioned "fall zone" 6 feet beyond most equipment. Swings should have more—twice the height in front and back, plus 6 feet on either side. Even those who scrimp on the area of cushioning should follow recommendations for depth, which the commission determined by dropping a metal "head" full of instruments. How much will it cost? Rubber mats are expensive—at least $10 per square foot installed. That leaves loose fill. A 6-inch blanket of bulk sand or pea gravel is one option. Several playground designers recommended hardwood chips. Use your common sense, too. Keep equipment low—under 5 feet if possible. And consider advice from Candice Stein, a landscape designer in San Jose, California. Because cushioning compacts where it's needed most, she suggests digging a hole 2 feet deep at the end of slides or other key spots, and filling it with cushioning.

Numbers are heights (in feet) from which a fall onto the given depth of material would probably not be fatal.

MATERIAL	UNCOMPRESSED DEPTH 6"	UNCOMPRESSED DEPTH 9"	UNCOMPRESSED DEPTH 12"	COMPRESSED DEPTH 9"	COMMENTS
Sand	5	5	6	4	Good for play but can attract cats. May compact, reducing cushion.
Pea gravel	6	7	10	6	Does not compact or rot, but awful to walk on. If gravel spills onto nearby lawn, it can be kicked out as hail of missles by mower.
Shredded wood	6	9	12	9	Knits into firm wood surface and stays put. Needs occasional topping off.
Mulch	7	10	11	10	Free in many communities. Must be replenished as it decomposes.

The proper site for a play structure relates to safety as well as aesthetics. Rock was blasted away at this site to create a safe pocket for play. The structure was designed by Matt and Libby Eliott, architects in Blue Hill, Maine.

[choosing lumber]

FROM YEARS OF EXPERIENCE, TOM SILVA KNOWS EXACTLY WHAT to look for when he buys wood. For many home owners, however, buying lumber is a mysterious process. Even at a well-organized lumber yard, the multitude of choices can bewilder a novice. "You need a trained eye," says Tom, "to distinguish the good boards from the bad." The challenge of finding the right wood increases with outdoor projects exposed to the weather. Sun and water are hard on wood; they'll easily exploit any flaw you offer them.

above all, *says Tom, avoid buying wet wood. Inexpensive meters are available for checking moisture, but Tom doesn't use one. "If I pick up a 2x4 and it feels unusually heavy," he says, "I know it's soaked."*

Over the years, Tom has seen a general decline in the quality of available lumber. "When I scan a piece," he says, "I look closely for loose knots, big knots, checks and cracks. I want lumber that is good and straight and has as few knots as possible, especially near the edges." Tom's purchasing begins with what he calls "shopping the ends." Out in the yard at Arlington, he carefully

Tom sights down a board to determine if it is warped, a technique that identifies problems right away. Though many lumber defects can be handled with careful placement of the wood, warp can be troublesome and is best avoided.

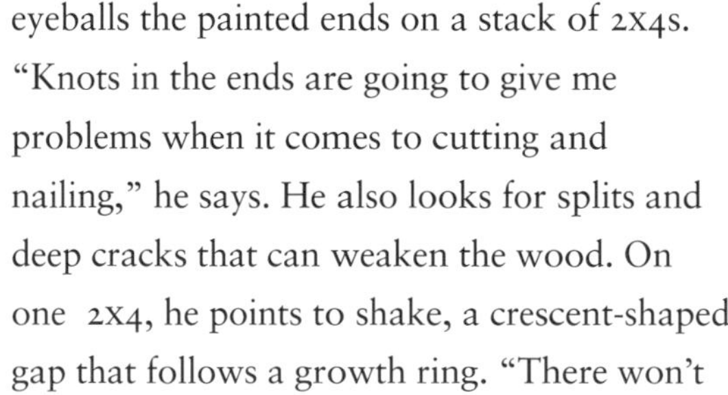

eyeballs the painted ends on a stack of 2x4s. "Knots in the ends are going to give me problems when it comes to cutting and nailing," he says. He also looks for splits and deep cracks that can weaken the wood. On one 2x4, he points to shake, a crescent-shaped gap that follows a growth ring. "There won't be much strength in this board," he notes.

Pulling a 2x6 from an opened stack, he lays his hand palm-down across the width of the board. "I can immediately tell by feel whether a board is cupped," he says. "It's tough to nail plywood to a stud that isn't flat from edge to edge." Warping along the length of a board can be troublesome as well.

When Tom sights down the edge of the 2x6, he discovers the wood is slightly arched from end to end. "This piece has a crown," he says, "If I were to use it as a stud, I'd have a pregnant wall." On the other hand, a 2x10 with a modest crown would make a good floor joist. With the apex of the crown arched upward, the joist would

Steel bands around the stacks help keep the lumber straight. Lumber should remain strapped until work begins. "When you take the steel bands off, there are always a couple of pieces that will warp and run wild," Tom says. "But a good lumberyard will let you return them." Paint on the board ends serves no practical purpose except to attract a buyer's attention.

[choosing lumber]

eventually straighten out and help prevent sag in the floor. "You just have to make sure you install the crown correctly," says Tom. "One time my brothers and I had finished building a deck when my dad noticed a dip in the floorboards. Sure enough, we had put in one joist with its crown going the wrong way, so it sagged like a swayback horse. He made us rip it out and turn it over. After that, I never forgot to check crown."

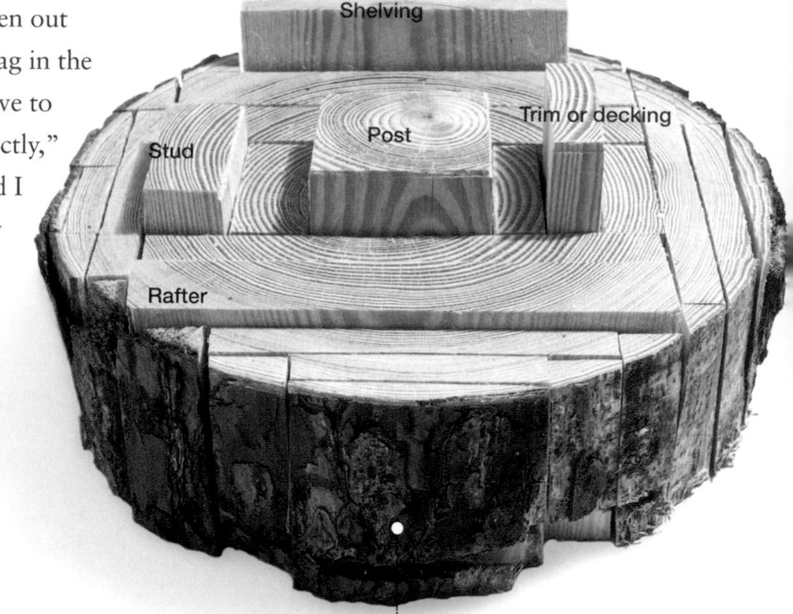

FLAT-SAWN LUMBER

QUARTERSAWN LUMBER

WHICH WOOD TO CHOOSE

No single tree species yields lumber with all the best characteristics at an affordable price, so Tom picks different woods based on their intended use. Standard 2x framing lumber doesn't need to be pretty, just strong enough and dry enough to hold up floors, walls and roofs. Tom once framed walls exclusively with fir: 2x4s for load-bearing walls and 2x3s for interior nonbearing partition walls. Now he orders No. 2 spruce, a weaker wood, but he uses wider stock: 2x6s for the exterior load-bearing walls, 2x4s for interior nonbearing

« Knots in the ends are going to give me problems when it comes to cutting and nailing. »

All these 8-foot 2x10s are graded as No. 2 lumber and should be strong enough for use as joists, despite being riddled with knots—weak points where the tree has grown around and encased branches—and other visible defects. Cosmetic defects include: 1. Pitch: Resin that has oozed to the surface. 2. Blue Stain: Discoloration caused by fungus. 3. Checking: Surface cracks commonly caused by drying stresses. 4. Pin Knot: Less than ½ inch in diameter. 5. Torn grain: Roughened surface where a planer or saw pulled wood out of the board instead of slicing it smooth. 6. Bark pocket: Encapsulated tree skin; not a problem if small. Structural defects include: A. Split: A cross-grain break all the way through a piece. B. Encased Knot: Growth rings are separate from surrounding wood. C. Knothole: A void left by a dead branch. D. Reaction wood: Grain that turns toward the edge. E. Intergrown knot: Shares growth rings with surrounding wood. F. Shake: A separation between growth rings. G. Spike Knot: An embedded branch, sawn lengthwise.

[choosing lumber]

walls. For deck and porch framing and for mudsills, where rot-resistance is paramount, he buys pressure-treated southern yellow pine. For exterior trim—soffits, corner boards, window casings and the like—Tom usually orders white pine in nominal 1x or 5/4-inch ("five quarter") thicknesses. And he makes sure to protect the wood from water before nailing it up. "Pine today doesn't have the tightness that it had years ago; you need to coat it on all six sides with paint." If the budget allows, he'll buy a more rot-resistant species like redwood or western red cedar. For porch decking, clear, vertical-grain Douglas fir is Tom's traditional choice. For uncovered decks, he has used redwood, cedar, pressure-treated yellow pine, and even Philippine mahogany, a tropical hardwood so dense it must be drilled before it can be nailed.

FLAT-SAWN LUMBER

Most lumber comes from logs that have been flat-sawn, producing boards with end grain nearly parallel to the face. The milling process is fast and yields a wide range of products—posts, framing lumber, boards—with little waste. Compared with quartersawn lumber, however, flat-sawn pieces are more likely to warp as a board dries or to blister paint with changes in humidity. Lumber is referred to by nominal dimensions, which are larger than actual measurements. For example, a 2x4 is reduced, by planing and drying, from a nominal 2 inches by 4 inches to 1½ inches by 3½ inches. The discrepancy increases as lumber gets wider than 6 inches. Hence, a 2x8 becomes a 1½ by 7¼. Lengths are not subject to this perplexing nomenclature: An 8-footer is actually 8 feet long.

QUARTERSAWN LUMBER

Dividing a log lengthwise into quarters is a slow and expensive milling process that produces lumber prized for its stability and beautiful grain. A board is sliced off one face of a log quarter, which is then flipped for a cut off the other face. On each board, the tree

Bending over a stack of 2x6s, Tom looks for knots, checks, splits and other defects in the board ends. If the boards will be trimmed later, some of these defects can be removed. But if he needs the full length of the board, Tom knows that such defects can lead to problems. Twisted and cupped boards, such as those on the facing page, can be difficult to spot in the stacks, however.

understanding a board

SAWMILLS MARK EVERY PIECE OF FRAMING LUMBER WITH A GRADE STAMP, WHICH INCLUDES IMPORTANT INFORMATION ABOUT A 2x's STRENGTH, GRADE, MOISTURE CONTENT, AND TREE SPECIES.

GRADE: THE MOST PROMINENT NUMBER OR LETTERS ON THE STAMP PRIMARILY INDICATE STRENGTH AND STIFFNESS, RANGING FROM THE HIGHEST QUALITY, SELECT STRUCTURAL (SEL STR), TO THE LOWEST, NO. 3 GRADE. TOM SILVA TYPICALLY ORDERS NO. 2 OR BETTER FOR MOST OF HIS FRAMING JOBS.

MOISTURE CONTENT: SURFACED GREEN (S-GRN) INDICATES A MOISTURE CONTENT OF 20 PERCENT OR HIGHER. SURFACED DRY (S-DRY) MEANS THE PIECE WAS AIR- OR KILN-DRIED TO A MOISTURE CONTENT OF 19 PERCENT OR LESS. MC 15 AND KD 15 HAVE MOISTURE CONTENTS OF 15 PERCENT OR LESS.

SPECIES OR SPECIES GROUPING: SPF=SPRUCE, PINE OR FIR. HEM-FIR=WESTERN HEMLOCK AND WHITE FIR, AMONG OTHERS. SYP=SOUTHERN YELLOW PINE.

GRADING AGENCY: THERE ARE 25 CERTIFIED GROUPS IN NORTH AMERICA THAT ENSURE, THROUGH SURPRISE INSPECTIONS, THAT MILL GRADERS HEW TO STANDARDS.

MILL NUMBER OR NAME: THE SOURCE OF A PARTICULAR LOAD OF LUMBER CAN BE LOCATED BY CHECKING BOARDS FOR A MILL IDENTIFICATION. THIS HELPS DISTRIBUTORS WITH QUALITY CONTROL.

rings run at nearly right angles to the face, so the wood is less likely to cup or twist. This premium-priced lumber, described as quartersawn or rift-sawn, depending on the exact angle of the end grain, is in short supply at most lumberyards but can be purchased by special order. "Anytime I want a board that won't expand and contract too much—on decking, flooring, trim—I look for that vertical grain," Tom says. "The wood is easy to work and holds paint well. Or, it looks great if you use a stain to show off the grain."

When Tom climbs out of his pickup at a favorite lumberyard, he pauses to breathe in the scent of freshly cut wood. Entering the open 20-foot-wide doorway of one of the yard's sheds, Tom heads down a truck-sized aisle. "This is where they keep wood that needs to be protected from the weather," Tom says. Vertical racks on the right hold lengths of Douglas fir for decking, yellow pine for moldings, and white pine for shelves. Horizontal racks on the left hold premium wood for interior and exterior trim, including redwood, white pine and poplar. "This is a beautiful piece for porch decking," says Tom, pulling a Douglas fir 2x4 off a rack. The board, golden-orange with straight vertical grain, is pristine except for a small black knothole on one edge. Taking out his tape measure, Tom checks the distance to the knot. "I could still get 10 feet of perfect wood out of this 14-footer," he says. "Or I could just lay the knot down against the joist. Nobody would ever see it." Choosing good lumber inevitably involves the art of compromise.

[small buildings]

WEATHERPROOF STORAGE FOR THE LAWN MOWER? An outbuilding to enhance the garden? With careful design and construction, a garden shed can be both. And once you master the basics of building small, anything is possible.

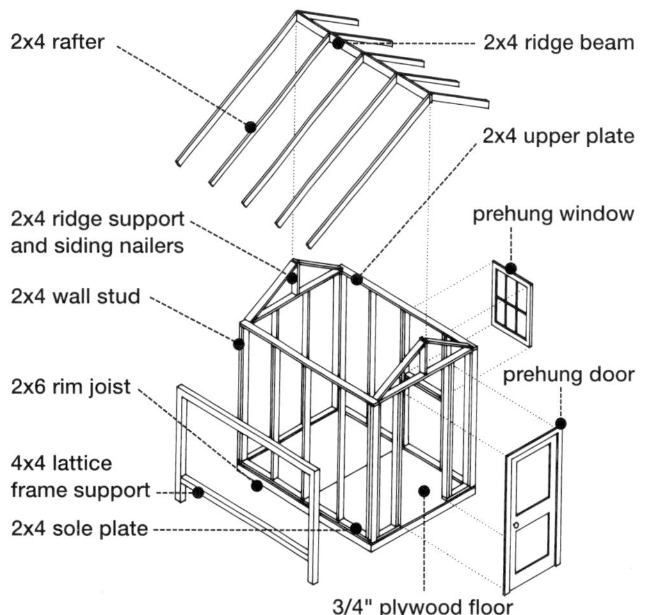

Nick and Susan Dazzo wanted a shed tailored to their garden and made of high-quality materials. *This Old House* enlisted the help of Les Walker, an architect who specializes in tiny houses. His plan took into account that the Dazzos are adventurous but not experienced do-it-yourselfers. Norm Abram provided long-distance advice; a local carpenter, John Gladdis, lent his expertise; and a small band of friends wielded hammers and paintbrushes. In three days they created a shed that is the pride of the garden. A gallery of ideas for creating other small buildings starts on page 101.

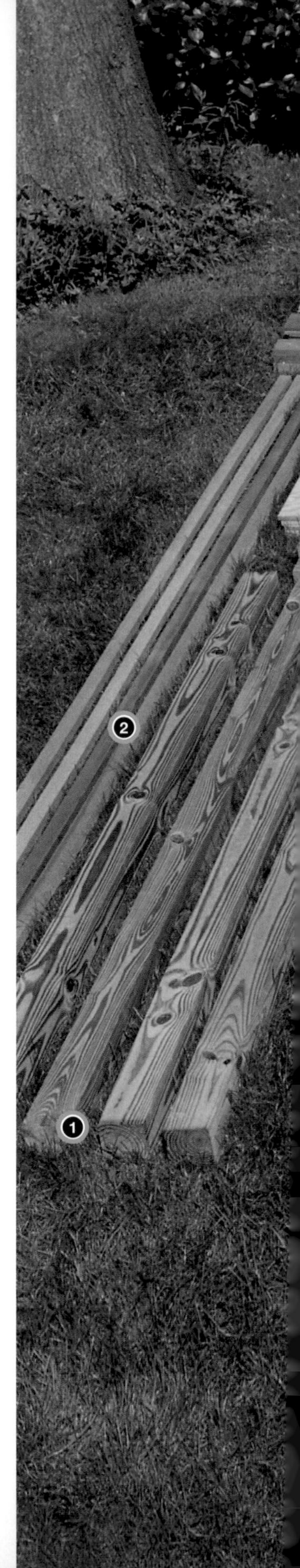

Materials list: 1. four 4x4 pressure-treated lattice frame supports, 8'; 2. four 1¼" x 1¼" batten strips, 12'; 3. four 2x2 pressure-treated ledgers, 3'10½"; 4. four 2x6 pressure-treated rim joists, two at 7'9", two at 6'; 5. five 2x4 pressure-treated floor joists, 5'9"; 6. fifteen H-3 hurricane anchors; 7. plywood: three sheets ⅝" ACX, 4'x 8' for roof; two sheets ¾" ACX, 4'x6' for floor; 8. nails: 10 lbs. 10d galvanized common nails; 10 lbs. 8d galvanized commons; 5 lbs. 8d sinkers; 5 lbs. 6d stainless siding nails; 5 lbs. 8d galvanized finish nails; 1 lb. 10d galvanized finish nails; 1 lb. 1" galvanized commons; 2 lbs. 4d galvanized commons; 9. four 1¼"x 1¼"x 12' cedar lattice stops; eight 1¼"x 4" cedar cornerboards, 8'; two 1¼"x 4" cedar roof trim (fascia), 8'; two 1¼"x 4" cedar roof trim (rake), 14'; 10. ½"x 6" cedar clapboard, 504 linear feet; 11. thirty 2x4 wall studs, 6'7"; four 2x4 wall plates, 5'4"; two 2x4 window liners, 3'6"; three 2x4 sills, 2'x8½"; six 2x4 braces, 8'; 12. eight concrete blocks, 8"x8"x 16"; 13. eight 5/16"x 6½" galvanized lag bolts with washers; 14. 8" aluminum flashing, 30' roll; 15. steel crimped ridge roll, 8'; 16. two 4x4 aluminum post bases; 17. ten 2x4 rafters, five at 3'11½", five at 7'11½", all precut at 60°; one 2x4 ridge beam, 8'; four 2x4 gable rafter nailers, 3'1"; two 2x4 ridge beam supports, 1'9"; 18. cedar lattice panel, 4'x7'4¾"; 19. six-light prehung barn sash window, 28"x28"; 20. four 2x4 wall plates, 8'; 21. canvas drop cloth; 22. paint: 2 quarts deck paint; 2 gallons primer; 2 gallons rubber roof paint; 1 gallon exterior paint; 2 quarts exterior paint, second color; 1 quart exterior trim paint; tray and roller; 23. one tube vinyl acrylic caulk; 24. brushes: 4" nylon; 2" angular sash; 2½" flat sash; 1½" nylon and polyester blend sash; 5-quart plastic pail; 25. two-panel 1¾" exterior prehung fir door, 2'8" x 6'6"; brass lockset; shims.

The total cost of the project, in 1995, was just over $2000. Lumber and material prices can vary considerably, however, from year to year, and from region to region. To find out what this project would cost you, take the materials list to a lumber yard and ask them to bid it as a complete package.

[small buildings]

TECHNIQUE

1 **Plan:** Decide where the shed will go. The Dazzos used posts, a section of lattice, and a drop cloth folded to the overall size of the shed, to mock up the building. Then get a construction permit from the local building department. Clear the building site of overgrowth.

2 **Mark:** Assemble the floor system by nailing rim joists and joists together. Brace the flooring with a 2x4.

3 **Locate:** Use the assembled floor system as a guide to positioning foundation blocks. Set blocks in gravel-filled holes. Use gravel as needed to level the floor.

4 **Install floor:** Dig a trough around the inside perimeter of the floor, set flashing at least 4 inches deep to discourage pests, and backfill trough. Back-prime plywood and nail in place with 8d sinkers.

5 **Erect walls:** Assemble walls flat, using 10d nails to spike through plates into studs, then tip walls into place and brace. This wall contains the window framing.

6 **Connect walls:** When all the walls are in place, nail them together at the corners.

[small buildings]

7 **Begin gable:** Attach 2x4 nailers (for siding) to underside of end rafters, then position, level, and nail ridge support into place. Do both gables, then install the ridge.

8 **Raise roof:** Install the rafters, being sure to check the level of the ridge as you go. Toenail end of rafter to ridge with three 8d common nails. Toenail one 8d common through the rafter and into the plate (a more secure connection will come later).

9 **Dig:** Dig holes for the blocks that will support the lattice posts. Cut each 4x4 to fit under a rafter, then cut the rest of the lattice frame. Predrill bolt holes using a ½-inch drill bit, then install lag bolts and tighten with a wrench. Double-check squareness of frame as you work. Nail post bases to blocks with masonry nails. Set lattice frame into place and nail to bases (4d) and rafters (8d).

10 **Secure rafters:** Nail hurricane anchors to rafters with 4d common nails.

11 **Sheathe:** Nail the roof sheathing to rafters with 8d sinkers 8 inches on center. Make sure sheets abut on the center rafter.

12 **Install trim:** Install trim with 8d finish nails: fascia (two nails in each rafter end); rake (nails 16-inches on center); cornerboards and door trim (as needed). Prime trimmed ends. Install battens with sinkers 8 inches on center, and ridge roll with 1-inch roofing nails. Caulk batten covering plywood joint.

13 **Fit door and window:** Install the door, shimming as necessary to maintain level and plumb. Nail with 10d finish nails; countersink and putty holes. Install window likewise. Prime all window and door trim.

11

10

12

13

[small buildings]

14 **Install siding:** Install the clapboards on the long sides of the building first, so any miscut boards can be used on the short sides. Make cuts with a circular saw and a fine-tooth blade. Nail the clapboards with 6d stainless siding nails, leaving a 4-inch exposure. Take care when hammering: Cedar is soft and you can dimple the surface with an errant hammer blow.

15 **Paint:** Paint the trim (semigloss white), the clapboard siding (tan), and the door and lattice (khaki). Paint colors were selected to match the house.

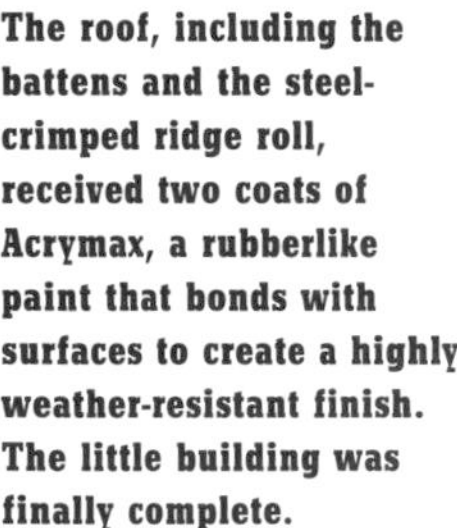

The roof, including the battens and the steel-crimped ridge roll, received two coats of Acrymax, a rubberlike paint that bonds with surfaces to create a highly weather-resistant finish. The little building was finally complete.

SOME PEOPLE CALL THEM DEPENDENCIES. OTHERS PREFER THE MORE PROSAIC "OUTBUILDINGS." BUT NEITHER WORD DOES JUSTICE TO THE INDEPENDENT SPIRIT AND ARCHITECTURAL SELF-SUFFICIENCY OF SMALL BUILDINGS, WHICH SIT SQUARELY WITHIN THE AMERICAN TRADITION. IN THE 18TH CENTURY, THE GROUNDS SURROUNDING A GRAND AMERICAN HOUSE WERE LIKELY TO BE DOTTED WITH A DAIRY, AN ICEHOUSE, OR A CHICKEN COOP. SOUTHERNERS, ESPECIALLY, LOVED OUTBUILDINGS. "THEY HAVE A QUEER WAY OF BUILDING ONE THING AFTER ANOTHER, THE GREAT POINT BEING TO HAVE A SEPARATE SHED OR OUT-HOUSE FOR EVERY PURPOSE," NOTED UNION OFFICER THEODORE LYMAN ABOUT THE REBEL PLANTER CLASS.

PROBABLY AS SOON AS THERE WERE "BIG HOUSES" THERE WERE LITTLE ONES, SAYS DON SWOFFORD, AN ARCHITECT IN CHARLOTTESVILLE, VIRGINIA, WHO SPECIALIZES IN HISTORIC PRESERVATION. LITTLE BUILDINGS DEDICATED TO DOMESTIC FUNCTIONS INCLUDED SPRING-HOUSES, LAUNDRIES, AND PRIVIES, EACH WITH A DISTINCTIVE SHAPE. BUT BY THE EARLY 20TH CENTURY, OTHER THAN TIN SHEDS, BARNS, AND GARAGES, OUTBUILDINGS PRETTY MUCH DISAPPEARED FROM THE LANDSCAPE.

IF OUTBUILDINGS ARE NO LONGER NECESSARY IN UTILITARIAN TERMS, THEY NOW SERVE A HIGHER PURPOSE. SOME CONNECT PEOPLE TO THEIR MUSE. WITH HER CARPENTER HUSBAND, LARS, ARCHITECTURAL DESIGNER ANNETTE LINDBERGH HAS CREATED A SERIES OF SMALL-SCALE GEMS, INCLUDING A ONE-ROOM CABIN IN THE WOODS (RECALLING AMERICA'S MOST FAMOUS SMALL BUILDING, THOREAU'S HOUSE ON WALDEN POND). "WITH THESE PROJECTS, I FEEL LIKE I'M GETTING BACK TO WHAT I DID AS A KID—CREATING PRIVATE HIDEAWAYS IN NATURE," SAYS ANNETTE. "THERE'S SOMETHING MAGICAL ABOUT A LITTLE HOUSE OF YOUR OWN."

outbuildings

[small buildings]

built up

TREEHOUSES ARE FOR KIDS AS WELL AS THEIR FRIENDS. WINNIE THE POOH HAS A TREEHOUSE, AND TARZAN DOES TOO.

PERCHED BETWEEN THE EARTH AND THE CLOUDS, TREEHOUSES LIGHT THE IMAGINATION AND FOSTER THEIR OWN KIND OF SUSPENDED ANIMATION. THEY ARE PLACES OF REFUGE, LAUNCHING PADS FOR DAYDREAMS, AND STAGES FOR FANTASY. CHILDREN TAKE TO THEM IMMEDIATELY.

THIS ONE COST ABOUT $1,000 FOR MATERIALS AND TOOK FIVE DAYS TO BUILD. IT ALSO TOOK A LEAP OF FAITH: THE TREEHOUSE IS ABOUT TWELVE FEET OFF THE GROUND, HIGH ENOUGH FOR A FALL TO BE SERIOUS. PETER NELSON, AUTHOR OF *TREEHOUSES: THE ART AND CRAFT OF LIVING OUT ON A LIMB*, SAYS IMAGINATION COUNTS, NOT GREAT ALTITUDE. "SIX FEET OR 60 MAKES NO DIFFERENCE. IT'S GETTING OFF THE GROUND AND INTO THE AIR THAT OPENS YOUR MIND, THAT BRINGS YOU IDEAS RIGHT OUT OF THE BLUE."

norm's pint-size victorian

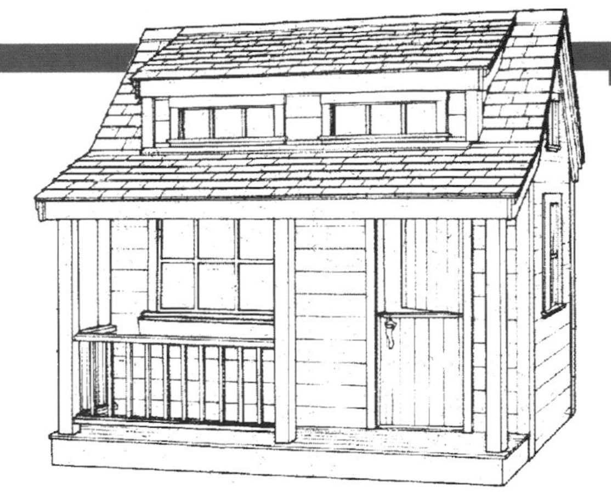

"ANYONE WHO CAN BUILD A DECK OFF THE BACK OF A HOUSE HAS THE SKILLS TO BUILD A PLAYHOUSE," SAYS MASTER CARPENTER NORM ABRAM. IN HIS NEW YANKEE WORKSHOP BOOK, *KIDS' STUFF* (LITTLE, BROWN), NORM PROVIDES PLANS FOR THIS 56-SQUARE-FOOT VICTORIAN. DESPITE SOME ELABORATE FEATURES—CEDAR ROOF SHINGLES AND TONGUE-AND-GROOVE SIDING, DORMER WINDOWS, A Z-BRACED DUTCH DOOR, AND A WINDOW BOX FOR FLOWERS—THE PLAYHOUSE TAKES JUST FOUR WEEKENDS TO BUILD. A MITER BOX AND A ROUTER WITH A FLUSH-TRIMMING BIT WILL MAKE THE WORK GO FASTER, BUT AN AMATEUR CAN GET BY WITH A CIRCULAR SAW, HANDSAW AND DRILL. MAKING A PLAYHOUSE SAFE FOR KIDS, NORM ADVISES, SHOULD BE THE PRIMARY CONCERN OF ANY BUILDER. PICK A SITE IN PLAIN VIEW OF THE MAIN HOUSE AND BE SURE TO USE UNBREAKABLE POLYCARBONATE "GLASS" FOR WINDOWS.

DON'T USE WOOD THAT HAS BEEN PRESSURE-TREATED FOR EXPOSED PARTS OF THE PLAYHOUSE. ROUND OVER BALUSTERS AND OTHER SHARP EDGES. SPACE THE PORCH RAILINGS 3 INCHES APART OR LESS, CLOSE ENOUGH NOT TO TRAP SMALL HEADS. TRIM THE NAILS USED TO SECURE SHINGLES, SO POINTS WON'T STICK THROUGH THE CEILING.

AS LONG AS YOU SUPERVISE, IT'S OKAY TO GET KIDS INVOLVED WITH HAMMERING AND PAINTING, BUT LEAVE POWER TOOLS TO THE GROWN-UPS.

[small buildings]

trash taker

THE AVERAGE AMERICAN PRODUCES ALMOST 3/4 OF A TON OF GARBAGE EVERY YEAR. MULTIPLIED BY A FAMILY OF FOUR, THAT'S A LOT TO HAUL TO THE CURB. THE TRASH SHED HERE, NORM'S DESIGN, OFFERS ONE WAY TO ORGANIZE THE PROCESS AND KEEP PESTS AWAY FROM THE CANS. A SHELF ALONG THE INSIDE BACK WALL EVEN OFFERS SPACE FOR SOME GARDEN TOOLS (FACING PAGE).

TONGUE-AND-GROOVE CEDAR SIDING SHEATHES THE SIDES AND DOORS FOR A CLEAN, UNCLUTTERED LOOK. THE DOUBLE DOORS ARE HELD CLOSED BY A SLIDE BOLT AND AN ASTRAGAL, A STRIP OF WOOD ON ONE DOOR THAT OVERLAPS THE OTHER. A DOOR ON THE RIGHT SIDE OPENS TO THE DIVIDED RECYCLING CLOSET. THE ROOF IS HIGH IN FRONT, GIVING ACCESS TO THE BINS AND LETTING RAIN-WATER AND LEAVES SLIDE DOWN THE BACK.

THE SHED WAS COMPLETED IN ONE DAY AT A TOTAL MATERIALS COST OF $540.

PROVIDED BY
DEPARTMENT
OF
PROTECTION

[raising a flagpole]

LONG BEFORE FIBERGLASS OR EXTRUDED ALUMINUM, CRAFTSMEN working in spar yards used lathes to turn wooden flagpoles—masts with landlubber destinies. Honoring this maritime tradition, flagpole terminology still twists nautical: Flags are raised by sheaves (pulleys) and halyards (ropes) that are secured on cleats. Some poles even have double or step masts, yardarms (crossbars) and gaffs (extra spars perpendicular to the yardarms).

Mike Gilligan of Gilligan's Flags and Poles in San Luis Obispo, California, still creates flagpoles the traditional way: from old-growth vertical-grain Douglas fir, which has enough tensile strength to withstand high winds. His custom-made poles taper up from a four-sided base to an octagonal transition piece and a traditional spar on top.

Although wood is the most historically authentic material for a flagpole, it is also the most expensive. There are less costly options. The best fiberglass poles have a UV-resistant finish and are constructed with the majority of fibers running vertically; fibers that run horizontally make the pole weaker and can cause failure. Fiberglass poles are available in various colors and are light, easy to install and maintenance-free. The rigging can be run inside the pole to eliminate the sound of slapping halyards. Most models do not make lowering easy, however. Single-piece aluminum poles are light, easy to install, and available with internal rigging, but some painted aluminum poles chip, leaving uncoated spots that may stain. The most durable

Pole-setting basics: **This project called for a foundation hole 30 inches deep and 24 inches in diameter, filled with concrete. After digging the hole, Norm shoveled in 6 inches of concrete, let it set for a few minutes and then droped in the anchor (1). After checking the anchor's alignment with a level, he filled the hole with concrete and troweled it smooth. "The alignment of the base really determines the alignment of the pole," says Norm. After the concrete set for 24 hours, Norm and Gilligan lifted the pole onto padded sawhorses and prepared it according to the manufacturer's instructions. Before screwing on the truck (the flanged top), Gilligan coated the inside and edges with silicone caulking for a watertight seal. He then fit the finial (2), a gold-toned anodized aluminum sphere in this case, into a ½-inch threaded hole in the center of the truck. Once all was ready, the men fitted the pole's base into place, loosely tightened one locking bolt, then hoisted it aloft (3). After a final check for plumb, Norm tightened all locking bolts and ran up a 50-star cotton bunting flag.**

finish is clear-coated brushed metal, which often looks incongruous against a white clapboard house. The sight of retracting buttons and joints on a telescoping aluminum pole may not enhance the elegance of a pole's silhouette, but they make the pole easy to raise or lower.

To install a flagpole, the first step is deciding where in the yard to put it. Tom Hennessy of Hennessy House, a distributor of flagpoles, recommends assembling a mock-up with PVC pipe and standard couplers. One person should hold up the pole in various spots so a second person can judge the effect from various vantage points.

By the time Norm and Gilligan finished a flagpole project they worked on together in California, the sun was setting. Although that's usually the time to lower a flag, both men trotted the pole across the lawn and slipped it into place. After tightening the bolt, Norm attached the flag. Everyone watched breathlessly as he pulled on the halyards. The flag zipped to the top, snapped to attention and then shimmied in the breeze against the orange-streaked sky.

Norm and Mike Gilligan install a 20-foot wooden flagpole. Ideally, a pole should sit on a knoll in a prominent place by the front door. To choose a pole's height, consider the following guidelines: 18 to 25 feet for single-story buildings, 25 to 30 feet for two stories, and 30 to 40 feet for three stories.

[building a barbecue]

WHEN THE BARBECUES FLARE UP EACH SPRING AND THE SCENT OF charring seasoned meat floats across America, it's a wonder how vegetarians keep their resolve. Even a burger broiled on a rickety hibachi has that primal, irresistible hunter-gatherer allure and a tang of genuine alfresco hospitality. But Dr. Paul Gotkin's family wanted something more than a primitive fire pit to grill the day's catch. So under a gazebo near the Gotkin's Florida swimming pool, masons Chuck and Paul Palazzo gathered the tools and materials they needed to build a cookout space. It would be more than a steel kettle on legs.

a barbecue *encourages guests to linger and hosts to cook well into the evening. Be sure to provide suitable lighting in the area—cooking by flashlight isn't much fun.*

For those who can afford such luxuries, there's no denying the appeal of these massive monuments to the joy of cooking outdoors. They provide broad expanses of countertop to set down a plate of burgers or basket of buns. Their supporting pedestals, whether built of brick or block, make a perfect all-weather storage space for mitts, tongs and other barbecuing accouterments. And unlike those movable feast-cookers that require bottles of propane or bags of briquettes—both of which have a way of running out when most needed—stationary grills can be set up to burn pure convenience: piped-in natural gas.

"This is not a barbecue; this is a kitchen," says Larry Malesky of the Fireplace & BBQ Center in nearby Coral Springs, Florida, and the designer of the project. The Palazzo brothers could have been building a miniature house, judging by the stubble of wire and pipe poking out of the gazebo floor: electric wires for the small built-in refrigerator and lights, water-supply and drain lines for the sink, a natural gas line for the drop-in grill. The structure cradling all these amenities is solid as a house, too. Eight feet long, built of concrete block and pavers covered with travertine tile, the barbecue was cemented to the gazebo's 6-inch slab, a sufficient foundation in frost-free Florida. Here the problems are salt air, moisture, bugs and rot. "Ten years ago, people built these out of wood, with tile tops," Malesky says. "But those don't last in the Florida climate. Half our business is replacing them." He kicked a loose block. "This'll last forever, with no maintenance."

Beneath a riverside gazebo in Florida, a no-rot, no-rust barbecue takes shape. Mason Chuck Palazzo created the structure from a heap of concrete block and a wheelbarrowful of mortar (see page 112 for the results). Some construction details, such as the foundation, vary with climate; check with your local building officials.

[building a barbecue]

A couple of hours after the project got underway, the Palazzo brothers stacked the 8-inch-thick block into a wall 55 inches high, tall enough to provide a 16-inch backsplash behind the 39-inch counter. They worked in companionable silence; each chore seemed to divide naturally and wordlessly into Chuck chunks and Paul portions. "Mud," Paul might say, and Chuck would know to drag some bags of mortar over to the wheelbarrow for mixing, while his brother laid out the barbecue's next element.

TECHNIQUES

1 Getting a good start: The first rule of masonry—to make sure that everything is plumb and horizontal—keeps Chuck Palazzo's mortar-stained 4-foot level busy.

2 Providing a hefty structure: By the end of the first day, the 8-foot-long pedestal is ready for countertops. In all, the project requires 88 pieces of block—both 4- and 8-inch-thick—and four bags of mortar.

3 Closing up: Solid concrete pavers, two feet square, form the base for the barbecue's countertops and grill. Chuck drops them into hummocks of mortar, then cuts an access hole (lower right in photo) for the gas line. Later, he'll open a paver to accommodate the sink.

4 Leveling the countertops: Rather than level the heavy pavers, Chuck waits a day for the mortar to set, then tops them with a level, 1-inch bed of stiff mortar.

5 Finishing up: The brutal look of block disappears under travertine tile, bedded in thinset adhesive. The next day, Chuck grouts the tile and sponges it clean.

With chalk and tape, Paul carefully marked out the location of the two end walls, so that Chuck, with deft slaps, flips, snicks and taps of his trowel, could skillfully build 4-inch blocks up to counter height. At the left-hand end, he installed a block with screened holes to ventilate the refrigerator. If the barbecue unit had been fired with bottled gas, the containment space for the tanks would have been ventilated too.

[building a barbecue]

When both the end walls reached countertop height, the Palazzos prepared additional supports for the countertop's 2-inch-thick concrete pavers. Against the back wall, Chuck mortared pilasters of cut block to counter height and cemented a piece of angle iron on top of them. Then he blocked up the barbecue's facade, leaving openings for the refrigerator and under-counter storage. Flat bar steel bridged the top of these gaps. On the steel and block, Chuck troweled a ridge of fresh mortar into which he pressed each paver, then he went back and filled all the paver joints. At this point, he didn't concern himself with making the pavers level—he planned to fix that later.

He set one paver down low, creating a recessed platform for the stainless-steel barbecue unit. "Watch the dust," Paul said with a grin, as he got ready to cut a 6-inch-square hole in the platform to admit the gas line. Sure enough, the instant his circular saw touched the paver, a gritty white cloud erupted from the diamond blade, enveloping him in a cementitious fog. In the counter itself, he cut a larger hole for the bar-sized stainless-steel sink. In fact, every exposed piece of metal in this installation, even the storage compartment doors, would be stainless steel. Nothing else survives the salt air.

The skeleton of the barbecue was finished. Now it needed skin and innards. Next day, when the mortar had set up, the Palazzos

The grill is gorgeous, but steaks won't sizzle without fuel. For natural gas, the piping of choice—and code, in most cases—is schedule 40 black steel pipe, a ½- to 1-inch conduit that has been used for about 100 years. (Copper tubing, usually not allowed for natural gas, is often permitted for propane.) Exterior pipe has to be buried, but usually just 12 to 18 inches deep—gas will flow even in the freezing northern winters. Connections, however, are the province of professionals.

sponged off the pavers and began leveling the countertops. They plopped hills of stiff, low-slump mortar on the counter and flattened them out with a 26-inch aluminum bar, working it back and forth.

The Palazzos could have encased the pedestal in stucco to match the house, but the Gotkins chose tile instead. So, starting with the countertop, Paul covered every exposed inch of his concrete and cinder-block creation with tumbled beige travertine accented with black pieces. He chose the accent positions with the eye of an artist, sitting back on his heels to study their placement.

After a day and a half, the tile was finished and the grill was dropped in. A fitter from the local gas company connected and tested the hookup. Installing and connecting a gas line is a job only for a licensed plumbing contractor familiar with the local codes—a mistake here could blow your house into a pile of rubble. (A gas utility is a good place to start looking for a qualified professional.)

Finally, the Gotkins had a perfect place to cook and entertain. Ena Gotkin thought the family would cook there at least twice a week. "I have a grill on the stove inside," she said, "but the food doesn't taste the same."

choosing a gas grill

IF LIFE SEEMS TOO SHORT FOR BUILDING A FIRE AND WAITING FOR COALS, THE QUICK ANSWER IS A GAS-POWERED GRILL. BUT WHICH ONE? THE FIRST DECISION—WHAT SIZE TO BUY—DEPENDS ON HOW MANY PEOPLE YOU EXPECT TO COOK FOR, HOW MUCH THEY EAT AND HOW MUCH YOU WANT TO SPEND. GAS GRILLS RANGE IN WIDTH FROM 24 TO 65 INCHES AND IN PRICE FROM A FEW HUNDRED DOLLARS TO NEARLY $4,000 FOR A HIGH-END COOKER WITH EVERYTHING, INCLUDING AN INFRARED ROTISSERIE.

THESE READY-ANYTIME GRILLS BURN EITHER NATURAL GAS FROM A PIPE OR LP (PROPANE) GAS SUPPLIED BY A TANK. THEIR BURNERS ARE RATED IN BTUs. LARRY MALESKY OF THE FIREPLACE AND BBQ CENTER SAYS 15,000 BTUs PER BURNER IS THE MINIMUM FOR GRILLING: "THE HIGHER THE BETTER TO SEAR IN THE JUICES. IF YOU GO BELOW 15,000, YOU'RE THROWING YOUR MONEY AWAY." WHEN SHOPPING FOR BTUs, BE SURE TO COMPARE APPLES TO APPLES. SOME MANUFACTURERS ADVERTISE THE HEAT PRODUCED BY THE ENTIRE GRILL SURFACE (THEY MULTIPLY THE NUMBER OF BURNERS BY THE BTUs PER BURNER), WHICH GIVES THE IMPRESSION OF A SIGNIFICANTLY HIGHER OUTPUT. IF POSSIBLE, WANGLE A TRY-OUT INVITATION FROM GAS-GRILLING NEIGHBORS.

[digging a lilypond]

A WATER GARDEN CAPTURES SKY AND reflects its light back to the landscape. There is sound and movement from a fountain or waterfall and fish swimming among the water lilies. Nothing attracts birds like water—particularly moving water. They will perch on the rocks to drink and bathe in the shallows. A pond requires attention, but no other garden feature will be as rewarding.

When Rolf Nelson decided to build a lily pond in his Texas backyard, he called on his friend Richard Koogle of Lilypons Water Gardens. First the men outlined the pond on the ground with a garden hose and checked the shape from a ladder and second-story windows. A loose oval allows a future bridge or stepping-stones at the pinched area. The sod was cut with a spade and the hose removed. The excavated soil will be used later to create a berm to the north of the pond for plantings.

Rocks on one edge of this pond were set in mortar and arranged with a 3-inch overhang that casts a shadow on the water for a deep, natural look. Soil was backfilled to sandwich the liner against the rocks; the excess liner was trimmed flush. The original fill water, made alkaline by the mortar, was siphoned out and the pond was refilled.

When some elements of nature are missing, they can be added. Local stone set into a shallow shelf around the pool edge provides a rustic counterpoint to the mirror-flat surface of the water. Almost any pond requires some maintenance—stones can topple over, and debris can collect on the bottom—but a properly planned body of water largely takes care of itself.

[digging a lilypond]

TECHNIQUES

1 Plan the shape: Outlining the shape with a garden hose is an easy way to mock up a naturalistic shape. The larger the pond, the more digging it will require. Now is the time to think carefully.

2 Level the edges: To keep water from spilling out one end or the other, scrape soil from high areas and add it to low ones, then check your work with a level taped to a long, straight board.

3 Detail the excavation: This pond will be rimmed with flat stones and steel lawn edging, resulting in a natural but neat look. The stones will be set into a shallow trench.

4 Place the underlayment: Matting around the sides of the pool and sand on the bottom keep any remaining sharp stones and roots from damaging the liner, which will follow.

5 Haul in the liner: After the liner was hefted into place and spread out, the pond was filled with water only to within 4 inches of the top, so that finishing work from the inside would not cause overflow.

The hole should have a flat bottom and gently sloping sides. Experts recommend making 12-inch-deep shelves on which to set potted, shallow-water plants, and digging the rest of the area down to at least 18 inches for water lilies. To level the pond edge, soil was scraped from high areas and added to low ones. To size the liner, the pond was estimated as a rectangle 16 by 6 feet (widest dimensions). To assure that the liner would be big enough, the depth (18 inches) was multiplied by 2½, and the resulting 45 inches added to both length and width.

In keeping with the pond's naturalistic shape, Nelson and Koogle decided not to make a formal "necklace" of coping stones around the rim. They will use them only on the north side, closest to the house, to blend in with a future rock garden. Using local stone and making the edge as natural as possible will avoid the planted-pool look. On the north side, the men dug a shallow trench for flat stones; on the south, they installed steel lawn edging. The liner will go under the rocks on one side and over the edging on the other, where it will be trimmed off 4 inches beyond the rim and buried beneath sod.

Matting and sand protect the liner from sharp stones or roots that might puncture it over time. A synthetic felt-like underlayment fabric was cut into panels to fit the sides, but old carpet can also be used. Liners come in many sizes and are made from materials such as inexpensive PVC or more costly, longer-lasting rubber. Thicker liners last longer—up to 50 years. To avoid damage, the liner was folded into a strip and carried to the hole, then unfolded and allowed to settle. Creases were, where possible, gathered and smoothed. The pond was partially filled with water, which pressed the liner against the sides of the pond, making the creases barely visible.

A pond should not be sited in a low place where runoff from the property can foul the water or dislodge the liner. Nelson wanted water lilies in his pond, so it had to be located in full sun—away from the shadow of the house and overhanging tree limbs. This also eliminated the need to dig around tree roots and reduced leaf clean up. The pond is the focal point of a new garden area, which will eventually be reached by a stepping-stone path from the house. It's not a good idea to install a lined pond where the water table is high or the soil drains very poorly—hydrostatic pressure might shift the liner. You will have to deal with drainage. One way is to make a 1-foot-wide, gravel-filled channel under the pond, running along its length. Start it 6 inches deep at one end and increase the depth ½ inch per foot until it extends at least 3 feet beyond the opposite end. The channel should lead to a gravel-filled dry well.

On the north edge, rocks were set in mortar and arranged with a 3-inch overhang that casts a shadow on the water for a deep, natural look. Soil was backfilled to sandwich the liner against the rocks, and the excess liner was trimmed flush. The original fill water, made dirty and alkaline by the mortar, was siphoned out and the pond was refilled. Water lilies were placed on the lowest part of the pond floor and shallow-water plants set on the shelves. Soon, life will join the garden.

siting a pond

IF YOU WANT TO BUILD A "NATURAL" POND, A BEAUTIFUL SPOT ISN'T THE ONLY CONSIDERATION. "I'VE HAD LOTS OF HOME - OWNERS POINT AND SAY, 'I WANT IT RIGHT THERE,'" SAYS BILL WHITEHOUSE, AN EXCAVATOR FROM WOODSTOCK, VERMONT. "HALF THE TIME, THAT AREA JUST ISN'T RIGHT FOR A POND." BEFORE MOVING A SHOVELFUL OF DIRT, WHITEHOUSE—WHO'S BEEN BUILDING PONDS FOR 16 YEARS—LOOKS FOR WATER, WHETHER IT'S AN UNDERGROUND SPRING, A STREAM, OR A SO-CALLED HIGH WATER TABLE. WITHOUT A NATURAL SOURCE, A POND CAN'T HOLD WATER YEAR-ROUND. NEXT, WHITEHOUSE DIGS TEST HOLES TO FIND OUT HOW DEEP THE SOIL GOES BEFORE HITTING BEDROCK.

THE IDEAL WATER DEPTH IS 6 FEET OR MORE. IF IT'S LESS, HE'LL NIX THE SPOT OR IMPORT MATERIAL TO BUILD THE DAM—A COSTLY ENTERPRISE. AT THE HOLES, WHITEHOUSE TESTS THE SOIL CONTENT FOR CLAY AND SILT BECAUSE THEY PACK WELL AND HAVE LOW WATER PERMEABILITY. THEN, ASSUMING THE AREA PASSES LOCAL, STATE, AND/OR FEDERAL APPROVAL, WHITEHOUSE STRIKES UP THE BAND AND DECLARES THE AREA A SUITABLE POND SITE. "IF YOU WANT A NICE POND, YOU'VE GOT TO DO IT RIGHT," HE SAYS.

[bocceball court]

BECAUSE PATRICIA Marvin grew up with seven brothers and sisters, married into an Italian clan, and has four children, she qualifies as an expert in the demanding art of staging get-togethers. "If you have a family, a big family, you know how it goes," she says. "You might go long periods where you don't see any of the relatives. Then you seem to see them almost too often. It gets to where you're asking: 'What have you been doing—in the last two weeks?'" Gathering everyone for any event is a major production.

One year, she contemplated the string of upcoming graduations for her son and daughters, and the celebration that she and her husband, Ron, wanted for their own 25th wedding anniversary. Their acre of woods, lawn and deck just north of Boston began to seem somehow inadequate. "I sure don't want more lawn," Patricia remembers thinking as she pondered how to pep up the place. The Marvins ruled out a basketball court (a magnet for jocks but useless to others), horseshoes (fun but not for little kids) and a swimming pool (too much work and too much worry that a child might drown). But bocce, they thought, bocce is beautiful.

The basic game is so simple that even kids can play after just a few minutes' instruction. Each team tosses or rolls four softball-size

While waiting for a load of stone dust, contractor Ralph Dellatto (right) puts a corner to good use. A clutch of balls (left) represents the many incarnations of bocce. Clockwise from top: an Italian design that blurs into stripes as it rolls; a slightly elliptical lignum vitae antique for bowls, the English game; stainless steel, for the French *pétanque;* a wooden palline, the target in bocce; brass, required by one international bocce federation; and plain plastic.

[bocceball court]

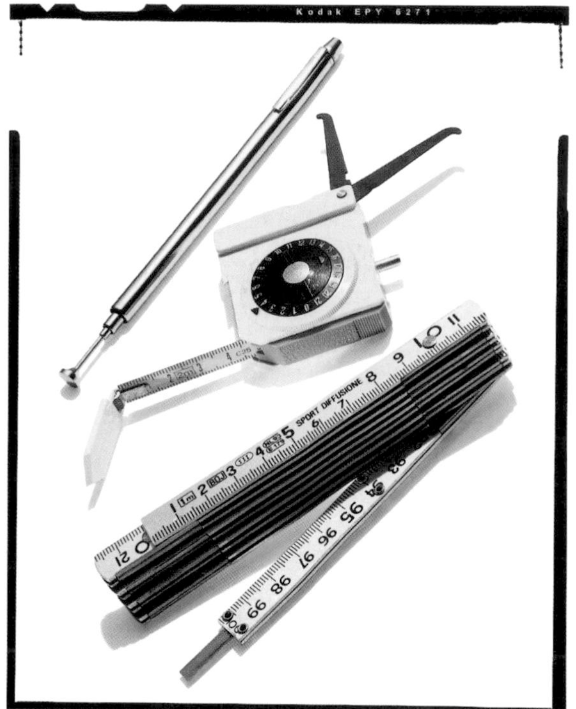

It takes rugged tools to scoop out a bocce base (above). Intending to make room for 3 inches of gravel and 6 inches of stone dust—standard insurance against a soggy court—the crew later skipped the gravel due to fast-draining soil. Later, players will use finer tools (left) to measure point balls.

balls so they wind up as close as possible to the target pallino, about the size of a squash ball. The game challenges participants to loft shots of 50 to 70 feet that land within 2 feet of the target. But most important, from the perspective of backyard players, is the "very significant social interaction to this game," says Ken Dothée, who headed the U.S. Bocce Federation for eight years. "Your competition is standing right next to you and, as often as not, you're playing over a glass of wine. Or maybe you're discussing the upcoming weekend while the barbecue is warming up."

Patricia called Ralph Dellatto, a general contractor who grew up playing bocce. The Marvins' court was Dellatto's first, so he bought a couple of books and the Marvins gathered some advice from knowledgeable players. Patricia's first plan called for leveling part of a slope at one side of the backyard, but Dellatto calculated that earth-moving alone would be a significant expense. Instead, he and his son, Daniel, built the court in a flat part of the yard. "By putting it there, we cut the cost right in half," Ralph Dellatto says.

A court must, above all, be level and firm.

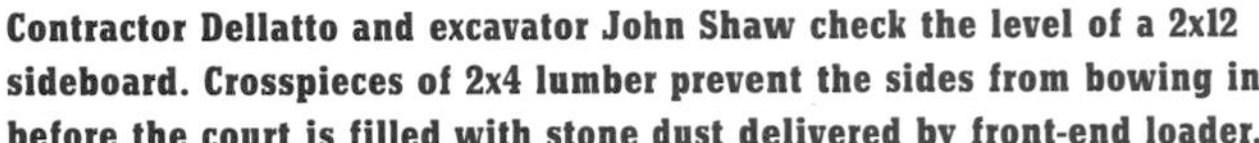

Contractor Dellatto and excavator John Shaw check the level of a 2x12 sideboard. Crosspieces of 2x4 lumber prevent the sides from bowing in before the court is filled with stone dust delivered by front-end loader.

Raking fills in areas that the front-end loader couldn't reach. Next, the surface will be compressed by a mechanical roller to reveal low spots, which are filled with more stone dust. After a final rolling, the court is ready.

"You want to make sure you have a surface that is relatively hard and will remain such with minimum maintenance," Dothée says. "Don't put in sand—you will almost guarantee a soft court. You may be able to wet it and pack it down and play one game, but at the end of the day you will have a soft court again." Crushed oyster shell, ground limestone, and granite and stone dust from quarries are all popular because their sharp edges make them pack better than sand, which is rounder. "It's what's indigenous to your part of the country. In Italy, they use powdered marble."

Court size varies considerably, too. The International Bocce Association stipulates a court size of 12 by 60 feet. The U.S. Bocce Federation recommends the court size used in international play: 27.5 by 4 meters, roughly 91 by 13 feet. For their court, the Marvins stretched out garden hoses until they found boundaries that looked right. They settled on a court 12 by 60 feet, aligned with their deck and within view of the kitchen window.

The construction took two days. A month later, Ron's family came over to celebrate his birthday and inaugurate the court. Children played first, then the old men. After that, it was a jumble of kids, moms and dads. Patricia says the court accomplished everything she had hoped: "It brought out the athlete in everyone." And it opened up a whole new dimension of conversation as well as a lot of different topic areas. Without a doubt, bocce was in their blood. Which perhaps explains why it wasn't until after dark that anyone noticed the Italian feast that had been sitting untouched for hours. Only then did everyone's attention shift from the court to the table.

bocce

is an ancient game. As early as 5000 B.C, the Egyptians played a form of bocce using polished rocks.

[framing a trellis]

"A PHYSICIAN CAN bury his mistakes," said Frank Lloyd Wright, "but the architect can only advise his clients to plant vines." Vines hide a multitude of sins. They obscure ugly views, disguise downspouts, link unrelated windows, conceal pipes and utility boxes, and can turn architectural "mistakes" into vertical gardens. Don't they damage buildings, eating mortar and prying up clapboard? Not if properly chosen and properly supported.

anticipate *the eventual need to remove a trellis for maintainence, house painting, or repair.*

There are vines for quick cover, like the annual morning glory, and herbaceous vines that die to the ground each year and return again to cover a trellis in one season, like golden hops. But most of the climbers we crave are woody: English ivy, climbing hydrangea and wisteria. These plants will be around for decades, so design them into the garden as if they were elongated shrubs. Be patient—they can be slow at first. Then stand back. There's an old gardener's saying that compares vines to babies: first year sleep, second year creep, third year leap. That's exactly how it works.

TECHNIQUE

Kip Anderson cuts lattice pieces with a miter saw. To figure length, he starts with two 4-inch overhangs, then adds the number of openings that fit on the wall and ¾ inch to allow for the width of the final crosspiece.

1 Square: He uses a square to align pieces at one end and clamps them so he can mark all horizontals in one pass and verticals in another. On horizontal pieces, he marks the best face.

2 Mark: Vertical pieces are marked on a finger-jointed side but rotated for assembly so a more attractive side will face out. An X shows where the crosspiece will lie.

3 Drill: To conceal screws, he drills and countersinks holes into the backs of the verticals, at roughly the center of intersections. A scrap piece is underneath.

4 Assemble: Kip assembles the trellis from the back on a large, flat surface. He lays the horizontal pieces face down (marks up), then lays the verticals on top and drives 1¼-inch all-weather screws into each joint. He starts at a corner, then works all the way down one side and across the bottom to keep pieces steady.

1

2

3

4

[framing a trellis]

5 Trim. He trims the edges of a redwood 2x4 at an angle, then cuts it to the width of the trellis to make a supporting cleat. Generally two are needed, one near the top of the trellis and one near the bottom. The cleat is attached to the wall so that it slopes downward and sheds water away from the building. Kip drills two shank holes and ½-inch counterbores on the outside edge of the cleat, locating them so they will hit studs inside the wall.

6 Attach. Kip attaches a cleat to the wall with 3½-inch screws, then screws trellis verticals to the cleat with 2-inch screws. The finished trellis (above) awaits its vines.

Kip Anderson, gardener for public television's *Victory Garden*, makes trellises out of redwood grounds: finger-jointed lengths of stock, sometimes sold at lumberyards as thickness guides for plasterers. Sturdy and rot-resistant, grounds are relatively inexpensive. Openings need not be square; rectangles work too, says Kip, but 8- to 10-inch spacing usually looks best. This trellis has 7¼-inch openings—8 inches counting the ¾-inch stock.

how they climb

VINES ARE MOST LUSH IN THE SOUTH, BUT THEY WILL GROW IN ANY STATE OF THE NATION. ANNUALS WILL GROW FOR ONE SEASON, BUT IF YOU WANT A PERMANENT VINE, CHOOSE ONE THAT IS HARDY WHERE YOU LIVE. HARDINESS REFERS TO A TOLERANCE OF AVERAGE MINIMUM TEMPERATURES.

MOST VINES TWINE TO CLIMB TOWARD THE SUN. WHEN THE STEM MEETS AN OBSTACLE, CELLS GROW FASTER ON ONE SIDE, CAUSING THE STEM TO WIND. OTHER PLANTS, LIKE CLIMBING ROSES, SEND UP SHOOTS THAT GET TANGLED IN TRELLISES OR SIMPLY REST ON SUPPORTS. SOME PLANTS, LIKE GRAPEVINES, CLIMB WITH TENDRILS—MODIFIED LEAF STEMS THAT TWINE AROUND SUPPORTS. A FEW, LIKE THE PASSIONFLOWER, EVEN PRODUCE CURLY SPRINGS ALONG THE TENDRILS THAT ACT AS MINATURE SHOCK ABSORBERS TO CUSHION THE VINE'S WEIGHT AND RESIST WIND.

VINES LIKE IVY AND CLIMBING HYDRANGEA HAVE MODIFIED ROOTS OR ROOTLETS ALONG THE STEMS THAT GROW INTO THE ROUGH SURFACE OF SUPPORTS; OTHERS, SUCH AS BOSTON IVY, DEVELOP DISKS LIKE TREE-FROG TOES ON THEIR ROOTLETS THAT WILL EVEN STICK TO SMOOTH SURFACES.

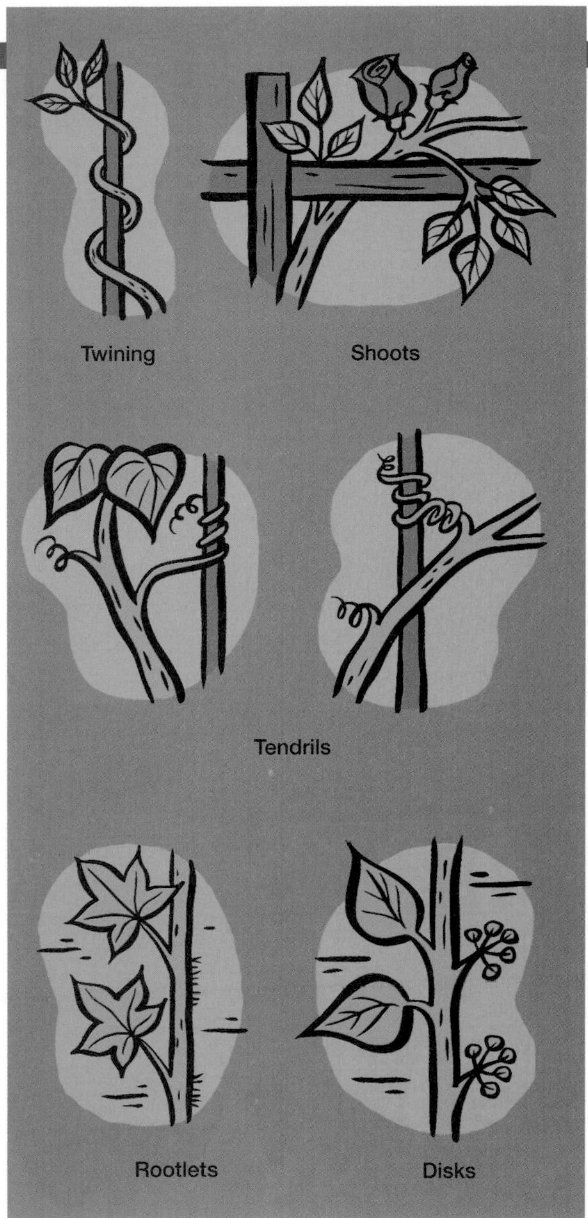

The clematis (pronounced *klem*-a-tis) is the queen of all climbers. There are hundreds of varieties, climbing from 3 to 30 feet, with flowers that range from 1 to 10 inches across. Plants bloom, depending on variety, from spring to fall. This is a Clematis viticella hybrid, which climbs using leaf tendrils.

[outdoor shower]

FROM THE CHILDLIKE BLISS OF A COLD-WATER HOSE ON A HOT day to the rapture of a long, warm, wet bombardment, showering alfresco is one of life's great underreported pleasures. It turns duty into adventure, the morning shower into an exclamation point of delight. Purely a summer activity in some locales, outdoor showers are possible year-round in moderate climates.

At one vacation house in Rosemary Beach, Florida, an attractively simple shower provides the basics. "It's a nice place to rinse off the sand before you go upstairs," says contractor Burrell Elliott, whose crew built it just steps from the dunes. Architect Eric Watson designed the 3-by-5-foot shower on a deck at the house's northwest side. For the enclosure, he specified 3½-inch-wide pine pickets weatherized with a dark brown stain to match the exterior trim of the house.

Before the wooden deck was built, plumber Carl DeLong laid underground copper supply pipes, installing shutoff and drain-down valves inside the house's garage, next to the water heater. (For outdoor showers that must be winterized, Richard Trethewey, the plumbing and heating contractor for *This Old House*, recommends hot and cold shut-off valves inside the house, plus a drain-down valve outside in the shower. "That way, you turn the water off inside, turn it on outside, and the pipes drain themselves," he says.)

Inside the little shower chamber, carpenter Mike Smits built a narrow wooden box to house the piping and valves, and DeLong fitted pipes together, ensuring they were the right distance apart to go unnoticed between the pickets. Then DeLong put in a single-lever pressure-balanced shower valve. If a toilet flushes somewhere in the house, the valve automatically adjusts to the pressure to avoid scalding the person showering. Richard Trethewey says every shower, indoors or out, should have such valves. DeLong agrees. He also agrees that, ideally, a showerhead should be placed at a height of about 6½ feet.

Elliott conceded that, despite the wood's smoothness and its two coats of mildew-retardant stain, traces of mold might have to be scrubbed off periodically. There was no concern about clogs; the shower would drain into the sand. Smits finished nailing the pickets on all three sides of the shower. Spaced 1½ inches apart, they let the pleasing breeze pass through—a much higher priority than privacy for this shower, intended for rinsing sand off swimsuit-clad bathers after a visit to the beach. Morin swiped on more brown stain and the shower was complete, save the final test. Smits switched on the water, and it sprayed out beautifully, splashing across the deck and onto the hot sand.

Building an outdoor shower calls for close coordination between carpentry and plumbing craftsmen. Once the structural frame of the shower was in place, the carpenter (left) lined up pickets under a leveling stick, at a height of 5′ 9″. Then the plumber jumped in (right). Here, he installs a foot-wash spigot, an ideal device for rinsing sand-caked toes.

Tucked under a stairwell balcony, the completed outdoor shower (far left) is ready to douse salty, sandy beach-combers. A 5-inch diameter-showerhead, twice the size of most fittings, provides a generous spray for cleaning up.

good drainage *is essential in an outdoor shower. Standing water breeds mosquitoes and can smell. Make sure sunlight and the breeze can dry out the stall to discourage algae and mold.*

WOOD SCULPTURE: courtesy carpenter ants

[decksandfences]

TWO DAYS AGO, THERE WAS nothing but DIRT and detritus. NOW, SANCTUARY SEEMED tangible.

[outdoor woods]

AMONG BUILDING materials, wood is just about perfect: beautiful, strong, easily shaped, and renewable. Unfortunately, it is also vulnerable to decay and insect attack. Before chemical preservatives came on the scene, builders controlled the damage by selecting lumber from trees that had natural resistance to such deleterious effects (or by slathering the wood with smelly solutions such as creosote). Redwood and cedar are the most common rot-resistant woods still in use, but longleaf pine, black locust, red mulberry, Pacific yew and several others can be found as well. Builders, however, now have additional choices, and nearly one-fifth of softwood boards and timbers sold get their rot-resistance from chemical preservatives. What wood is best for yard projects? The answer, alas, is "It depends." Following, a guide to the choices.

CEDAR

The cathedral-like silence of the British Columbian forest is shattered as logger Jack Currie fires up his chain saw. The object of his attention—a Western red cedar four feet across—has stood on the spot for more than 200 years, surviving fires, windstorms and insect attacks. It will take just 20 minutes for Currie to make the undercut and back cut that will lay low the 180-foot giant.

For 5,000 years, Western red cedar (*Thuja plicata*) has been growing along the moist margins of the Pacific coast, from northern California to southern Alaska, and inland to the western slopes of the Rockies. Under ideal conditions, a red cedar can live 1,000 years or more and reach heights of up to 230 feet. The native people in the Pacific Northwest built houses and canoes with this evergreen's aromatic wood, turned its shaggy gray bark into clothing and medicine, and made baskets with its tough roots. So valued was the red cedar that they called the tree "Long Life Maker."

Modern builders also value red cedar's cinnamon-colored wood for its ability to withstand weather, rot and pests. Though its soft, open-celled structure makes cedar less than ideal as a framing material, it is perfect for shakes and shingles, for lining saunas or for decking and exterior trim. Because of its high concentrations of thujaplicin, a natural fungicide, the wood is exceptionally hardy.

Paint is the simplest "treatment" for outdoor wood, but it must be properly applied. This fir baluster was painted only after damage began. By then the raw wood had become a wick, sucking up moisture.

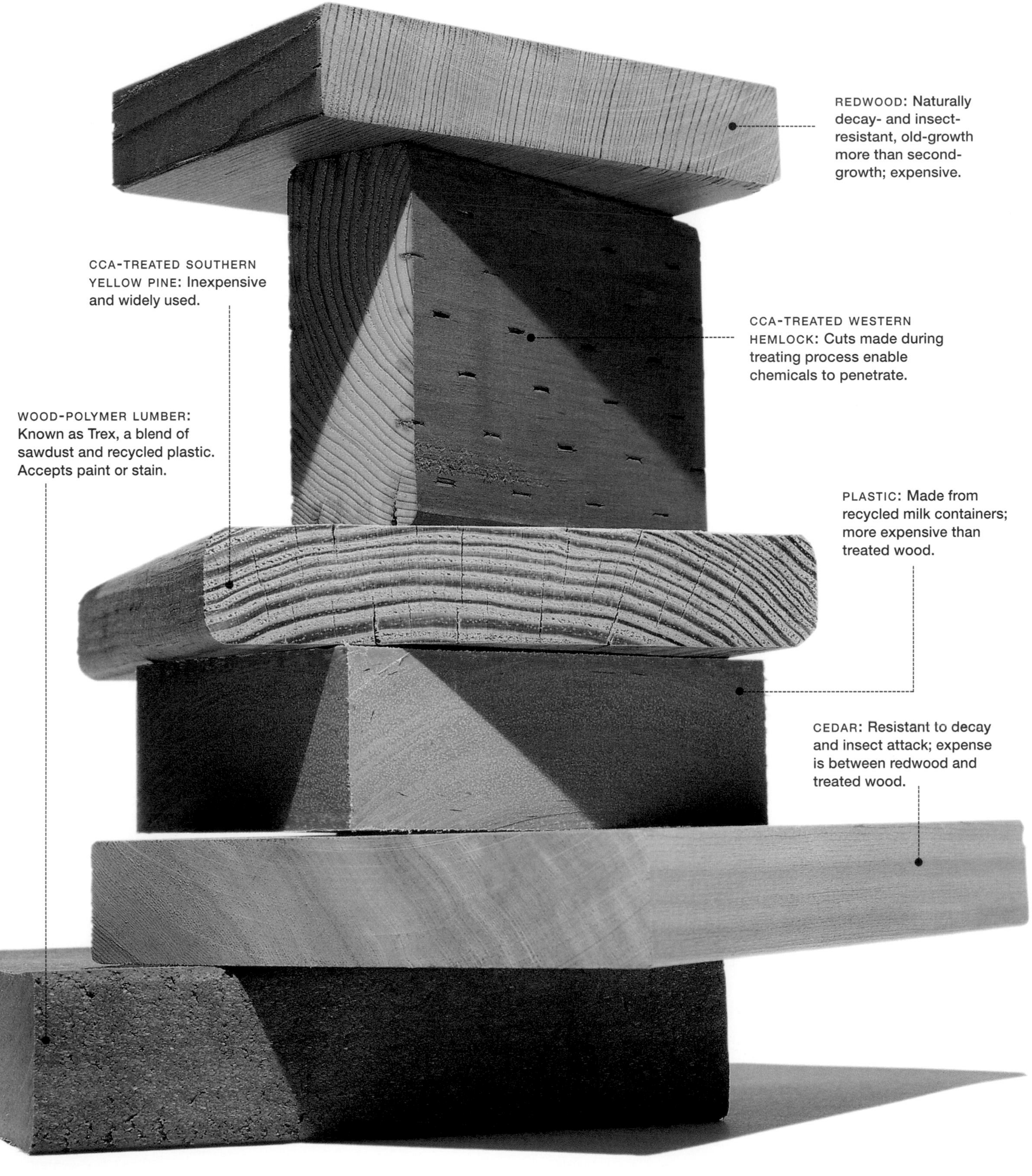
REDWOOD: Naturally decay- and insect-resistant, old-growth more than second-growth; expensive.
CCA-TREATED SOUTHERN YELLOW PINE: Inexpensive and widely used.
CCA-TREATED WESTERN HEMLOCK: Cuts made during treating process enable chemicals to penetrate.
WOOD-POLYMER LUMBER: Known as Trex, a blend of sawdust and recycled plastic. Accepts paint or stain.
PLASTIC: Made from recycled milk containers; more expensive than treated wood.
CEDAR: Resistant to decay and insect attack; expense is between redwood and treated wood.

Sound cedar trunks have been found on the forest floor 100 years after they fell.

His cutting finished, Currie puts aside his saw and inserts a pair of plastic wedges into the back cut. Four or five solid whacks with the back of his ax and the old tree trembles, cracks and falls in a whistling rush that shakes the earth. Trailing a measuring tape, Currie climbs up onto the felled trunk and begins cutting off branches and "bucking," or sectioning, the log into the 42-foot lengths preferred by the mill. It will take him and his crew a few days to cut down every tree in the area. Then a grapple yarder and loader will collect the fallen logs and pile them on trucks for the trip down the Squamish valley to the dry-land sorting yard, where each log is scaled, graded and sorted by species.

Eventually, the logs will be tied into bundles and dropped into nearby Howe Sound, where tugs will nudge them into quarter-mile-long log booms for towing to highly automated mills laced with the spicy scent of cedar. There, the logs will be stripped of their bark and efficiently turned into siding.

Within the year, the clear-cut from which the cedar was taken will be replanted or allowed to regenerate naturally. "Second-growth" trees will reach harvestable size in 60 or so years. But it is doubtful such trees will yield wood of the quality found by logger Jack Currie. "I'd be lying to you if I said the trees from a 60-year stand have the same quality as 150-year-old trees," says Gordon Prescott, a planning forester with Empire Logging in Squamish. With only enough old growth left for another 50 years or less of logging, according to the Ministry of Forests, prime cedar lumber is going to become an ever more scarce—and more expensive—commodity.

With the decimation of old-growth cedar tracts in the United States and subsequent bans on logging on public land, British Columbia now has the world's largest remaining reserves of mature Western red cedar stands—an estimated 1.1 billion cubic yards. The province is trying to exploit and protect this resource at the same time—not an easy task.

Unlike in the United States, where 28 percent of forests are publicly owned, nearly 94 percent of British Columbia's timber is on

With a thundering crash, a venerable cedar (left) begins its journey to lumber stardom. The butt end of a more than 200-year-old log (right) shows the rotting center characteristic of old cedar trees. Even so, plenty of good wood can still be milled from this log.

[outdoorwoods]

lands controlled by the provincial government. Logging companies are granted long-term timber farm licenses, and the government takes an active role in making sure its forests are properly managed. It even runs a central seed bank and experimental nursery for cedar and other trees. Up to 12 million nursery-raised cedar seedlings are replanted each year; 85 percent survive.

So while it is clear that there will be cedar forests in the future, they will be different from the towering stands George Vancouver saw in the 18th century. Most will be young and as intensively managed and maintained as a field of corn, leaving what's left of the majestic old forests for parks and protected zones.

A massive cedar log thumps through the maw of a debarking machine, which slashes off the thin bark without harming the wood. Nothing is wasted in milling cedar. What doesn't become lumber or siding is chipped for paper pulp or burned to heat the drying kiln.

IPE

A relatively unknown wood, at least in the U.S., is a rock-hard, chocolate-colored Brazilian hardwood called ipe. It has a legendary reputation for durability (it covers the famous boardwalk in Atlantic City, for example). The 1x4 ipe boards Tom Silva used on the deck of the show's Billerica, Massachusetts, project (see page 149) have an estimated 40-year lifespan—nearly twice that of treated yellow pine—and cost Tom roughly as much as clear redwood. There is a downside to ipe's incredible density, however: It is impossible to hammer a nail or drive a screw through it without drilling a pilot hole.

REDWOOD

Before the middle of the 19th century, forests of redwood (*Sequoia sempervirens*) stretched like a patchy beard along a narrow band of coast from southern Oregon to California's Big Sur. The giant trees—the tallest of all living things—speared sunward 350 feet, and could grow to 22 feet in diameter. Bunched in dense groves of perpetual twilight, they had few enemies, other than high winds and old age. Even fire could not penetrate their thick, fibrous bark. When they finally fell, some had lived more than 2,300 years. Yet they could lie on the forest floor for centuries more, their heartwood nearly untouched by rot or insects,

A 136-foot-long redwood, 18 feet in diameter, felled in the early 1960s, yielded more than 71,000 board feet of lumber, enough to frame five average-sized houses.

sustainable redwood

WHEN PEOPLE TELL JASON GRANT THEY FEEL GUILTY USING REDWOOD, HE REMINDS THEM, "THERE ARE NO GOOD OR BAD WOODS, ONLY GOOD AND BAD FORESTRY PRACTICES." GRANT, A VICE PRESIDENT OF ECOTIMBER INTERNATIONAL IN BERKELEY, CALIFORNIA, STOCKS REDWOOD LUMBER FROM SMALL TIMBER COMPANIES WITH EXCELLENT RECORDS OF SUSTAINABLE FOREST MANAGEMENT. INDEPENDENT AUDITORS EXAMINE IN DETAIL HOW THESE COMPANIES MANAGE THEIR FORESTS. IF THEY MEET THE STANDARDS SET FORTH BY ENVIRONMENTAL GROUPS, THEY BECOME CERTIFIED. SAWMILLS STAMP SURFACED BOARDS WITH AN "SCS" OR AN "SW" TO REFLECT THIS, BUT DON'T STAMP ROUGH LUMBER. THE PRICE OF CERTIFIED REDWOOD IS THE SAME OR SLIGHTLY HIGHER THAN NON-CERTIFIED WOOD.

nursing rows of new trees on their decaying sapwood as clonal offspring sprouted from their shallow roots.

In the tightly packed groves, growing at a glacial pace, redwoods could only sustain branches in the top third of their trunks. As a result, their massive lower two-thirds were clear, pristine wood, some with as many as 40 growth rings to the inch. Then came the California gold rush in 1849, prompting a massive demand for lumber. In a little more than 100 years, an estimated 90 percent of the pre-gold rush trees were gone.

Still, many forests grew back. The seedlings and juveniles left behind during the logging onslaught shot up at an astounding pace. Unlike their light- and space-starved ancestors, these new trees grew bushy with branches and reached formidable, harvestable sizes—up to 130 feet tall and 3½ feet in diameter—in just 65 years. These young trees, however, yield a lesser-quality wood. Untempered by competition, much second- and third-growth wood has widely spaced growth rings—as few as 3 an inch—and an abundance of knots. Gone is the strength, beauty and rot-resistance of wood from their ancestors, but the heartwood of second-growth redwood is still more durable than many other softwoods.

[outdoorwoods]

Redwood owes its legendary rot resistance to fungicidal insect-repellent toxins called extractives, which give redwood's heart its characteristic tint. These polyphenolic compounds are produced in the actively growing whitish-colored sapwood that sheathes the tree; they gradually migrate inward. The lumber from younger, smaller trees also tends to have a higher percentage of sapwood, which is extractive-free. The better grades of heartwood are remarkably stable, hardly changing in dimension through great swings in humidity. Joints stay tight, boards don't cup and warp. All redwood takes and holds paint beautifully, but outdoors it first needs a primer coat all-round to stop "bleeding," the rusty stains that surface when water dissolves the wood's decay-resisting extractives. A primer will also hide the marked difference between the light-hued early wood and darker late wood in each ring. Treat redwood decks with water-repellent preservatives or pigmented penetrating oils as soon as the wood starts to lose its color.

cutting *pressure-treated wood outdoors over a plastic tarp allows the sawdust to be rolled up and disposed of at the end of the job.*

Left to weather, redwood naturally turns a soft, dark gray. Woodworker Julian Hodges of Berkeley, California, specializes in custom-designed garden gates, and delays the graying with penetrating oil sealers. "It starts off looking oiled, but then ages to a fairly intense brownish hue and stays there," Hodges says. But Albert Slendebroek, owner of the Lumber Baron lumberyard near Berkeley, says anyone who applies a penetrating finish is doomed to put it on again and again. Salesmen visit him every year to demonstrate new products that clean and finish decks. Slendebroek points to the gray redwood deck outside his office and tells them to pick a section and go at it. "As you can see," he says, "any finishes and sealers have all worn off and failed." Slendebroek advocates buying the best wood possible and just "letting it be."

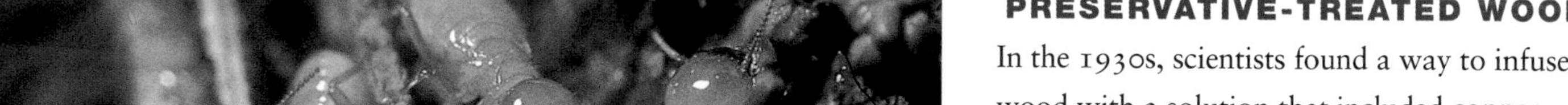

PRESERVATIVE-TREATED WOOD

In the 1930s, scientists found a way to infuse wood with a solution that included copper (toxic to the fungi that cause rot) and arsenic (then the most common insecticide). To ensure that protection would last and that builders and the environment wouldn't be hurt, they also added chromium, which triggered a chemical reaction that locked the pesticides into the wood.

Blind and nearly translucent, worker termites scurry for cover when exposed. They lack defenses against dry air or predators. Though they resemble ants, termites are more closely related to cockroaches.

what's under your deck?

THERE IS MORE THAN ONE WAY TO PRESSURE-TREAT PINE SO IT RESISTS ROT AND TERMITES. THE POST AT TOP RIGHT WAS INFUSED WITH A PRESERVATIVE FREE OF ARSENIC AND CHROMIUM BUT RICH IN COPPER, SO IT'S AS GREEN AS IF IT WERE TREATED WITH THE PROBLEMATIC ORIGINAL FORMULA. THE SAMPLE BELOW IT WAS PRESSURE-TREATED WITH ANOTHER ARSENIC-FREE PRESERVATIVE. IT WAS THEN SURFACE-COATED WITH A PRESERVATIVE STAIN THAT MIMICS THE LOOK OF CEDAR. HOME OWNERS CAN FIND OUT HOW MUCH ARSENIC IS UNDER THEIR DECKS FOR ABOUT $50. THE PROCEDURE IS SIMPLE: DIG A SPOONFUL OF SURFACE SOIL FROM 10 PLACES UNDER A DECK AND MIX THE DIRT IN A PLASTIC CONTAINER. PUT SOIL FROM OTHER PARTS OF THE YARD IN A SEPARATE CONTAINER. LABEL BOTH MIXES AND TAKE OR MAIL THEM TO AN ENVIRONMENTAL LABORATORY. "ANY LOCAL PUBLIC HEALTH DEPARTMENT SHOULD BE ABLE TO DIRECT YOU TO ONE," SAYS TONY BOGOLIN OF ECOLOGY AND ENVIRONMENT INC., A LABORATORY IN BUFFALO, N.Y., THAT ACCEPTS SAMPLES IN THE MAIL FROM ANYWHERE IN THE COUNTRY.

The formula became known as chromated copper arsenate, or just CCA. But the industry called it pressure-treated because the chemicals were injected into the wood under great pressure. The wood dried with a green tint because of the copper, but otherwise it was similar to ordinary lumber—except that it stood up to even the dampest, warmest climates. Indeed, stakes pounded into a termite-infested field at a federal laboratory in Mississippi in the late 1930s remain intact "and some of them will probably last 100 years," says Jerrold Winandy, a research wood scientist with the U.S. Department of Agriculture's Forest Products Laboratory in Madison, Wisconsin.

When the price of untreated redwood, cedar and fir soared, manufacturers of plantation-grown Southern pine seized on pressure-treating as a way to convert their product into one that would command a premium price, and sales of the greenish lumber ballooned. Virtually every piece of that wood carried a label stapled to one end, the manufacturer's guarantee against rot and insect damage. Dangling somewhere on each pallet was supposed to be another label with cautions required by the U.S. Environmental Protection Agency. The cautions are vague and mild: "Exposure to inorganic arsenic may present certain hazards...Do not use treated wood under circumstances where the preservative may become a component of food or animal feed."

But a single 12-foot-long 2-by-6 contains more than an ounce of arsenic. Though chromium and copper kill plants and marine life, arsenic presents the gravest danger to

[outdoor woods]

humans and many other forms of life. With the skyrocketing use of pressure-treated wood, 57 million pounds of arsenic is going into the backyards of America each year—nearly all of it reclaimed from copper and gold smelters in China and Chile. This presents an unsettling scenario: the United States as toxic waste dump of far poorer countries. No harm is done, however—as long as the pesticides remain locked in the wood.

In the late 1980s, researchers discovered that acids could reverse the chemical reactions that bind the pesticides. At the University of Guelph in Ontario, scientists soaked small cubes of the wood in a citric acid solution. Depending on its strength, the acid leached out 32 to 68 percent of the arsenic. Intrigued, a pair of researchers from the Connecticut Agricultural Experiment Station in New Haven decided in 1996 to crawl under decks to check whether acid rain—common in the Northeast—might be having the same effect. Analytical chemist David Stilwell and a colleague, Katja Gorny, sampled soil under seven decks, ranging from four months to 15 years old, and shared their results in the Bulletin of Environmental Contamination and Toxicology. In all cases, they found significantly higher levels of arsenic, chromium and copper than in soil collected away from the decks. The copper and chromium fell below state pollution limits, but the arsenic did not, and averaged 20 times higher than arsenic in surrounding soil.

These findings have prompted many people—including researchers at the U.S. Forest Service, which has long promoted pressure-treated wood—to take a fresh look at the material. Until Stilwell's study, scientists mostly worked with small samples of wood in laboratories—no one had ever studied the effect of acid rain on horizontal decking, where water is likely to pool and sink in. And the studies didn't factor in something that many home-owners now use routinely: chemical brighteners. Some of these contain oxalic acid, while others are made with citric acid—the same reagent that researchers at the University of Guelph used to induce leaching in samples of pressure-treated wood.

"The big risk with pressure-treated wood is that the arsenic will leach out and contaminate the groundwater, and then we will drink it," says Jerome Nriagu, an environmental chemist at the University of Michigan's School of Public Health and author of *Arsenic in the Environment*. Because the toxin occurs naturally in most soils, a small percentage of the nation's drinking water already needs special treatment, notes William Diamond, director of the Environmental Protection Agency's standards and risk-management division.

There is another problem. Although the chemicals in pressure-treated wood resist rot and many insects, they cannot protect it from weathering—or from the changing tastes of home owners. The Forest Products Laboratory estimates that pressure-treated wood will stay in use for 30 years. Retired from service, ordinary lumber can be mulched, recycled or burned to produce electric power, and its ash spread on crops as a nutrient. Not pressure-treated wood: Rather than destroying the arsenic, chromium,

be wary *of pressure-treated wood stamped "treated to refusal." The refusal zone of some species is just below the surface, leaving the inner wood unprotected.*

and copper, fire concentrates them in the ash. Burning even a small amount of the wood with other debris is enough to turn all the ash into hazardous waste.

Home-owners concerned about potential problems from pressure-treated wood face difficult solutions. Ripping out an existing deck just because it's there is costly and—in light of the growing waste problem—counter-productive. It makes more sense to seal the wood regularly with a moisture repellent. Paul Cooper of the University of New Brunswick, in Canada, says doing this will help lock in the toxic chemicals; manufacturers say it will also prolong the life of the wood.

Though there are alternatives to pressure-treated decking, pressure-treated posts and deck framing still makes sense—lives depend on rot-free supports. Tom Silva, general contractor for *This Old House*, has been using pressure-treated wood for years. "For sills and posts, it's a necessary evil," he says. "You feel a lot better being in a building or standing on a deck that is not rotting beneath you." He recommends using pressure-treated wood for all structural parts near the ground. This includes porch posts and posts installed in a crawl space.

Fortunately, suppliers of chromated copper arsenate have developed a new generation of chemical mixes: ammoniacal copper quartenary (ACQ), copper azole and copper citrate. In addition, other companies have recipes to protect wood without arsenic or chromium. The most heavily promoted is Kodiak Preserved Wood, made with copper dimethyldithiocarbamate.

The Environmental Protection Agency says these alternatives are safe, and the American Wood Preservers Association says they work. Three of them—ACQ, copper citrate and the Kodiak formula—are "pretty much one-to-one substitutes" for chromated copper arsenate, says Jerrold Winandy of the Forest Products Laboratory.

The new formulas cost more because they are richer in expensive copper. But wood and labor—not chemicals—are the most costly elements of wood-preserving, says Douglas Mancosh, president of BB&S Treated Lumber of New England. His company uses ACQ to treat a small portion of its wood, and he says the finished products cost 8 percent more than standard pressure-treated wood. Wood preservers could easily switch to arsenic-free formulas—using the same equipment and procedures—if consumers demanded it. "It's what I've been trying to argue for years," Mancosh adds.

Working with Pressure Treated Wood: An 8-by-10-foot expanse of pressure-treated decking contains 4 pounds of toxic metals (bottom right); that's the problematic aspect of some chemicals that keep decks looking great (top right). The Environmental Protection Agency advises sawing and machining pressure-treated wood outdoors. Workers should "wash exposed areas thoroughly" before eating, drinking or smoking, the agency says, and if sawdust accumulates on work clothes, they should be laundered separately. Protective gear is also advisable: Wear gloves when loading the wood (some carpenters prefer not to wear gloves when using power tools), and wear a dustmask when cutting it.

[building fences]

IN LYNN HIPPEAU'S PEACEFUL BACKYARD IN NEW CANAAN, Connecticut, the scene was anything but. Landscapers wrestled 12-foot-tall evergreens from a truck and dodged a growling skid-steer loader, pallets of bluestone and piles of crushed rock. A fencing crew lugged 6x6 cedar posts, V-grooved board sections, and panels of lattice to the edges of the yard, where workers dug holes, trimmed rails, tamped soil and persuaded posts with sledgehammers. Only 12 hours after this chaos erupted, a fence around the 3,000-square-foot backyard was already half-finished—60 feet of brilliant white gometry against brown earth and the rough edges of green shrubs.

"What you're striving for in any fenced garden is a serene, calm haven," says landscape architect Marc Schwartz. That is exactly the effect Hippeau asked Schwartz to design. The architect suggested arranging the yard into "garden rooms;" Hippeau wanted to follow principles of fêng shui, an ancient Chinese philosophy of placement. "It's not hocus-pocus, just good design," Hippeau says. Schwartz highlighted each roomlike area with fencing of lattice and solid boards. He specified lattice panels that extended from post-top to post-bottom and curved to match the edge of a nearby pool. A hedge of close-ranked arborvitae provided privacy. The rest of the 6-foot-high fence would be mostly solid panels of grooved shiplap boards topped with

At one end of the garden (left), five segments of 6-foot-high lattice fencing trace a broad arc against a living screen of shrubbery. The rails supporting the lattice panels were steam-bent and cut at at the factory.

Like the perfect hat for an elegant suit, a post cap completes a fence's appearance and sheds water away from vulnerable end grain. This cap is cedar, but caps in copper and other metals work well too.

[building fences]

2 feet of square lattice. In the center of the fence's longest side, marking the transept of the garden, Schwartz threw in another curve, a graceful latticed arch atop a panel of solid boards. He flanked this centerpiece with narrow, all-lattice sheets punctuated with an oval-framed window. Fêng shui aside, the final fence looked anything but Chinese and could have complemented any Victorian's backyard.

To project manager Robert Booth and his crew, however, niceties of design hardly mattered. They were there to build—fast and well. Long before the first hole was dug, Booth had started on the project by measuring the fence lines and marking off the post centers and gates. He delivered these dimensions, along with Schwartz's plans, to Walpole Woodworkers in Walpole, Massachusetts. Six weeks later, 27 posts, 24 panels and two gates arrived on a flatbed truck.

Like all Walpole Woodworkers fences, this one was milled from number-one northern white cedar, which naturally resists rot. The shiplapped boards between posts are ¾-inch thick; the lattice is ⅝-inch thick, not the ¼-inch-thick variety usually found at home centers. Rustproof stainless-steel staples secure each lattice crossing. All other nails and screws are galvanized. Before delivery, each piece of wood is coated with solid acrylic latex stain. When Booth and his crew first arrived at the site, they stretched a mason's line along the ground and staked off the centers of the post holes. Then they started digging. On most jobs, the crew excavates with muscle-powered shovels, less disturbing to the site and the ears than gas-powered augers. "We do it so fast and with so little mess—people think our fences were dropped out of the sky," Booth says. He'll call in a skid-steer loader with a hydraulic auger if the soil is too hard or rocky, but in Hippeau's sandy soil the digging was easy. The short-lever, pivoting-blade shovels they used reached the recommended 34-inch depth for 6-foot posts in minutes. (Posts 8 feet tall need 42-inch holes.) Heightening the "dropped out of the sky" illusion, shovelers

the fence, *in urban areas, usually marks the end of the property line. An important rule of thumb, however, no matter where you reside: Don't assume anything.*

Mahogany | Cast iron | High-density polyurethane | Hemlock

AT THE WALPOLE WOODWORKERS MILL IN CHESTER, A TINY VILLAGE ON THE FRINGE OF MAINE'S VAST NORTH WOODS, FENCE PARTS BEGIN THEIR JOURNEY TO SUBURBAN ESTATES AS LIMBLESS TREE TRUNKS IN A MUDDY STORAGE YARD. HERE, SOME 4,000 CORDS OF TREE-LENGTH WHITE CEDAR ARE SORTED, STACKED AND GRADED EACH YEAR. LARGE LOGS BECOME SQUARE POSTS, SMALLER ONES BECOME RAILS, AND THE SMALLEST GO THROUGH THE GANG EDGER, WHICH RIPS THEM INTO SEVERAL PICKETS AT A PASS. A MACHINE SIMILAR TO A GIANT PENCIL SHARPENER GIVES PICKETS THEIR FINISHED POINTS. TWO TRIPS THROUGH THE TWIN SAW, RIGHT, TURN A LOG INTO A POST. THE VINTAGE 1932 PLANER, A SCREAMING 9½-TON BEAST POWERED BY SEVEN MOTORS, SMOOTHS ANY STOCK UP TO 6 INCHES THICK AND 15 INCHES WIDE.

PERHAPS THE MOST INGENIOUS MACHINE IS THE SCARFING SAW. ITS BELL-SHAPED BLADE, LIKE THE DISK OF A FARMER'S HARROW, SWINGS IN AN ARC, CUTTING RAIL ENDS SO THAT THEY LOOK AS THOUGH THEY WERE HEWED WITH AN ADZE.

THE FINAL GRADING IS RUTHLESS: THE CHESTER MILL SHIPS ONLY NUMBER-ONE STOCK TO ITS SISTER FACTORY IN WALPOLE, MASSACHUSETTS, WHICH THEN ASSEMBLES AND PAINTS THE PIECES. "WALPOLE'S INSTALLATION CREWS DON'T HAVE TO WORRY ABOUT HIDING THE BAD SIDE OF A FENCE BOARD," SAYS MILL MANAGER BOB HAYES. "AND YOU DON'T MAKE BAD NEIGHBORS."

made in maine

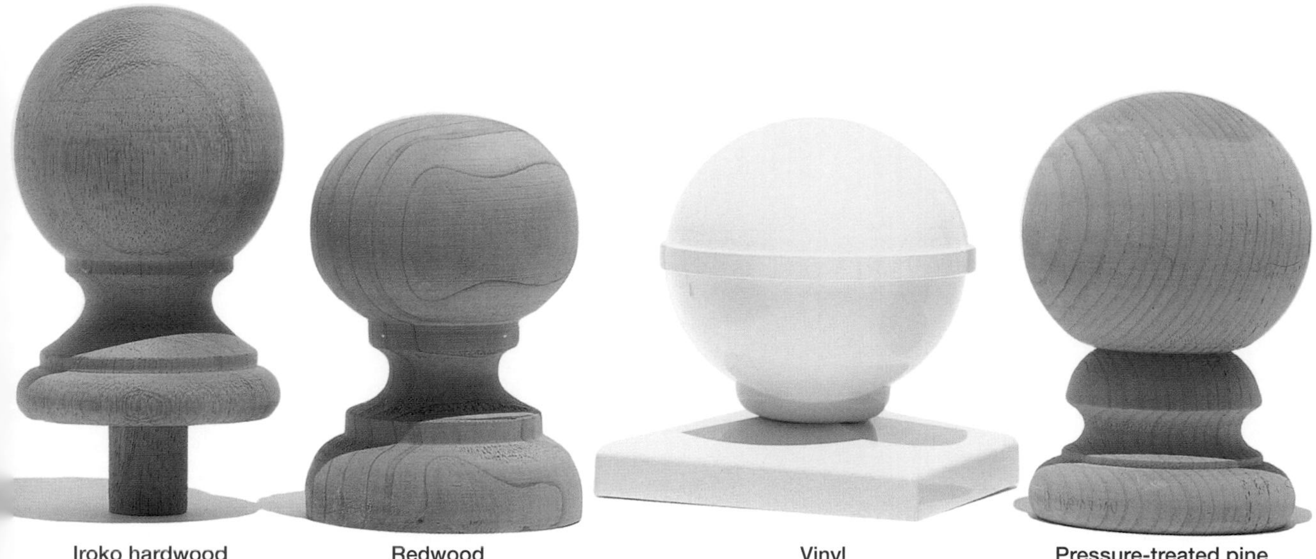

Iroko hardwood | Redwood | Vinyl | Pressure-treated pine

[building fences]

dumped their spoils onto canvas ground cloths to speed removal. "It's a lot easier to pick dirt up than pick it out," says crew member David Gladstone.

Tipped off a worker's shoulder, the first 40-pound post thunked into a hole. Then the post was jostled upright against the mason's line, plumbed with a 24-inch-long level and backfilled with the newly excavated dirt. Every 2 or 3 inches, a heavy steel tamping bar packed the fill solidly against the post. In most soils, Booth says, a thorough tamping anchors a post as effectively as a concrete collar does, and tamping is better for the wood. The crew almost never sets posts in concrete because water trapped between wood and concrete hastens rot and can burst the concrete if it

who owns a fence?

WHEN NEIGHBORS SHARE A FENCE ALONG A BOUNDARY, THEY ARE, BY LAW, CO-OWNERS OF IT. NEITHER PARTY MAY TEAR THE FENCE DOWN WITHOUT THE PERMISSION OF THE OTHER, AND THEY ARE EQUALLY RESPONSIBLE FOR ITS MAINTENANCE. (IF YOU CHOOSE TO PUT A BOUNDARY FENCE UP, HOWEVER, AND ARE THE ONLY PARTY WHO USES IT, YOU'RE SOLELY RESPONSIBLE FOR IT.) NEIGHBORS MAY MAKE THEIR OWN AGREEMENTS, PREFERABLY IN WRITING, REGARDING UPKEEP—E.G., ONE MAY AGREE TO LET THE OTHER CHOOSE A HIGH-QUALITY REPLACEMENT FENCE IF HE PAYS THE DIFFERENCE IN COST FROM AN ORDINARY ONE. BUT WHEN ONE NEIGHBOR MOVES, ANY PRIOR AGREEMENT IS NULLIFIED.

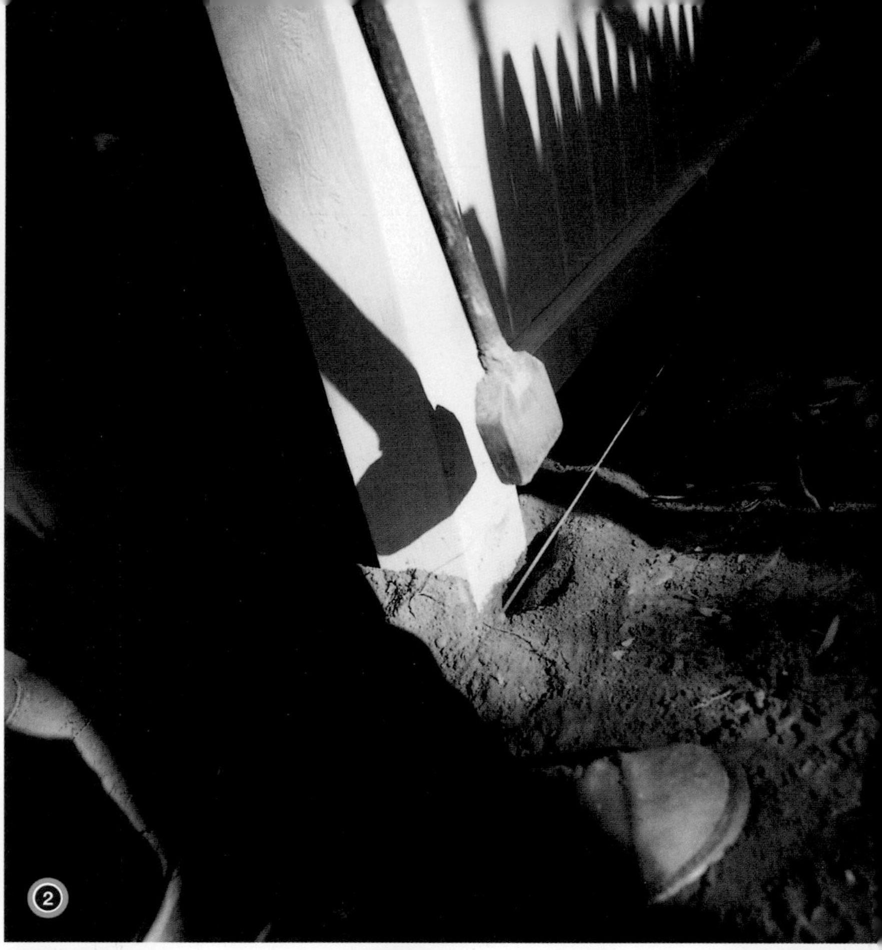

TECHNIQUES

1 Using the right tool: Crew member David Gladstone shuns traditional post hole diggers, which look like giant hinged chopsticks. His Gibbs Digger has a blade that swivels from vertical to horizontal with the flip of a short lever. Constant digging and sharpening wear the blade to a nub every nine months.

2 Tamping well: An iron tamping bar pounds the soil tightly around the post while it is held plumb. Porous soils make the best fence-post packing. About the only force that will lift a well-set post is a frost heave.

3 Focused persuasion: Banging on a post with a 5-pound sledge adjusts height quickly. The tool is also useful for leveling panels between posts. Care must be taken, however, not to overdo it: A post pounded too low must be completely redug and reset.

WITH ONE END STUCK IN THE GROUND, FENCE POSTS INEVITABLY SUCCUMB TO THE MICROBES THAT DESTROY WOOD. BUT THERE ARE WAYS TO SLOW ROT TO A CRAWL, SUCH AS CHOOSING THE RIGHT WOOD. BOB BOOTH, PROJECT MANAGER OF WALPOLE WOODWORKERS' FENCE DIVISION, USES ONLY CEDAR BECAUSE OF ITS ROT RESISTANCE. "IT CAN LAST 25 YEARS OR MORE," HE SAYS. HOME-OWNERS CAN FURTHER STRENGTHEN CEDAR'S ROT-RESISTANCE BY BRUSHING ON A PRESERVATIVE SUCH AS COPPER NAPTHENATE. AND AFTER A POST IS SET, THE DIRT AROUND IT SHOULD SLOPE AWAY TO DIVERT WATER. SIZE MATTERS, TOO: INSTEAD OF THE 4x4s USED TO ANCHOR MOST FENCES, WALPOLE USES 6x6s.

CONTRARY TO WHAT MANY BELIEVE, SETTING A POST IN CONCRETE DOES NOT ENSURE LONGER LIFE. AS THE WOOD DRIES, IT SHRINKS AWAY FROM THE CONCRETE, CREATING GAPS FOR WATER THAT PROMOTE ROT. ODDLY ENOUGH, ANOTHER THREAT TO POST LONGEVITY COMES FROM STRING TRIMMERS, WHICH ARE NOTORIOUS FOR GNAWING AT POSTS LIKE NYLON-TOOTHED BEAVERS. THE BEST DEFENSE? MULCH OR STONE PLACED IN A TIDY RING AROUND THE POST, SAYS *THIS OLD HOUSE* LANDSCAPER ROGER COOK. "IT'S THE BEST WAY TO KEEP GRASS AND WEEDS AWAY FROM THE WOOD," HE ADDS. "THAT ALSO MAKES A POST MORE MOWER-PROOF, ESPECIALLY WHEN YOU HAVE ONE OF THOSE BIG YARD TRACTORS."

post prescriptions

freezes. The workers pour concrete only when the bottom of a hole isn't deep enough to hold a post securely.

The next step is to attach the grooved board panel to the post. Paired wedges, 5½ inches square and 18 inches long, hold the panel a few inches above the ground as the crew fastens one end to the post with three 3½-inch galvanized wood screws. As the panel hangs from the post like a stiff flag, the next post is dropped into a hole, snugged up to the string and the panel, plumbed and tamped. The foreman, Mike Sludock, checks that the panel is level, adjusts the wedges, and checks again before screwing the other end of the panel to the post. Like a tailor matching a plaid along a seam, Sludock makes certain the lattice pattern on each adjacent panel lines up before attaching the lattice tops—which hang over the grooved board panels—to the posts. Gladstone follows behind each completed section, nailing on ornamental post caps and brushing on a touch-up coat of stain.

Even for a fence with as many different elements as this one has, installation is essentially the same basic sequence—dig a post, attach a panel, dig a post, attach a panel—over and over. The crew's skill shows when conditions at Hippeau's property call for a little improvising. For instance, when the panels must align at different heights because of sloping terrain, workers tack the lattice top up before installing the boards, to ensure that at least one horizontal strip aligns with its neighbor. When they discover that shrubs are planted less than a foot from the fence, they rearrange the post holes to avoid damaging root balls. When a post is bowed, they purposely set it so it bends away from the panel. Then they take a tie-down strap similar to those used by truckers and loop it to the nearest post. A few cranks on the strap's ratchet draw the offending timber upright long enough to screw the panel home.

As the afternoon light wanes, the crew packs up its tools. Sludock steps back to assess the day's progress. He counts 13 newly set panels. Although a three-man crew can often place 15 to 20 panels in a day, 13 is a lot on this site. Schwartz is pleased to see in solid form something that had only existed in his mind's eye. Two days ago, there was nothing but dirt and detritus. Now, with the crisp walls circling the yard, sanctuary seems tangible. And for him there is a surprise. The curving white lattice set against the dark-green screen of arborvitae makes the small backyard look more expansive. "That's an idea I'm going to steal for my future projects," he says.

A fallen tree is a dramatic agent of fence destruction, but rot, animals and even weed-whackers are the more common enemies. In this case, however, repairs were straightforward. After the fallen tree was hauled away, the damaged fence section was removed. Posts can often be extracted after pushing back and forth repeatedly to loosen soil. New posts and a replacement fence section followed.

[hands on deck]

BUILT TO LAST WITH robust materials and water-shedding details, Dick and Sandy Silva's new deck offers a commanding view of the pool, fish pond, and the thick woods behind the house. But what's immediately apparent to a visitor stepping onto the deck is its rich, dark wood—firm as stone and utterly free of knots—and the airy cedar pergola overhead, with its ever-changing play of shadow and light (for more on pergolas, see page 156). And beneath this deck's deceptively straightforward design lies Tom Silva's inventive, no-nonsense building methods. "I've torn down too many decks that were falling apart after just seven or 10 years," says Tom. "That's not going to happen with this one." It's a deck built for durability.

To that end, he's using durable materials and innovative techniques that can withstand decades of wet weather. "Water is the enemy," Tom says, and his defenses against it are as rigorous as those around a medieval castle.

For instance, Tom put half-inch blocks behind the ledger—the pressure-treated 2x10 that holds the deck to the house—to keep water from being trapped there. And instead of relying on traditional metal flashing to protect the plywood sheathing from melting snow and splashing rain, he applied a rubbery sheet of bitumen-impregnated plastic typically used on roofs. He ran it over the top of the foundation, behind the ledger, and 3 feet up the sheathing. *(continued on page 152)*

Decks offer terrific opportunities for outdoor entertaining. Only a safe deck is really a good one, however. Secured to the side of the house with bolts, this double-tiered redwood deck (left) can accommodate a crowd.

THE DECK TOM BUILT FOR HIS BROTHER DICK ILLUSTRATES THE BASIC ELEMENTS OF DECK CONSTRUCTION.
EVERY DECK MUST HAVE A FOUNDATION, AND HERE IT'S A SERIES OF 12-INCH-DIAMETER CONCRETE COLUMNS ATOP CONCRETE FOOTINGS (SEE PAGE 155) THAT REACH BELOW THE FROST LINE. HOW DEEP THE FROST LINE IS DEPENDS ON THE SEVERITY OF YOUR WINTERS; CHECK WITH LOCAL BUILDING OFFICIALS. ADDITIONAL SUPPORT IS PROVIDED BY A BEAM BOLTED INTO THE SIDE OF THE HOUSE (SEE PAGE 150). CENTERED IN THE TOP OF EACH COLUMN IS A METAL FRAMING-ANCHOR; IT CAN BE JABBED INTO THE WET CONCRETE OF A JUST-POURED COLUMN, OR FASTENED LATER WITH MASONRY ANCHORS AND CONCRETE SCREWS. AN ANCHOR CREATES A STRONG CONNECTION BETWEEN COLUMNS AND SUPPORT BEAMS—IN THIS CASE, TRIPLED 2X10S.
FLOOR JOISTS RUN AT 90 DEGREES TO THE BEAMS AND ARE TOENAILED TO THEM; DECKING RUNS 90 DEGREES TO THE JOISTS AND IS USUALLY FACENAILED TO THEM. IN THIS CASE, HOWEVER, TOM GLUED DOWN THE DECKING WITH A FAST-CURING, POLYURETHANE ADHESIVE USED IN THE BOAT-BUILDING TRADE.
THE SPAN (THE DISTANCE BETWEEN SUPPORTS) OF BEAMS, JOISTS AND DECKING IS DETERMINED BY THE TYPE OF WOOD, ITS DIMENSIONS, AND LOCAL BUILDING CODES.
ANY DECK THAT IS MORE THAN 30-INCHES ABOVE GRADE (MEASURED TO THE TOP SURFACE OF THE DECKING) MUST HAVE RAILINGS. HERE, SAYS TOM, NO RAILINGS WERE PLANNED BECAUSE THE GRADE WOULD BE BROUGHT TO WITHIN 30-INCHES OF THE DECKING. ALWAYS CHECK CODES FOR RAILING DETAILS, HOWEVER.

deck building basics

[handsondeck]

two good ways to attach a deck to a house

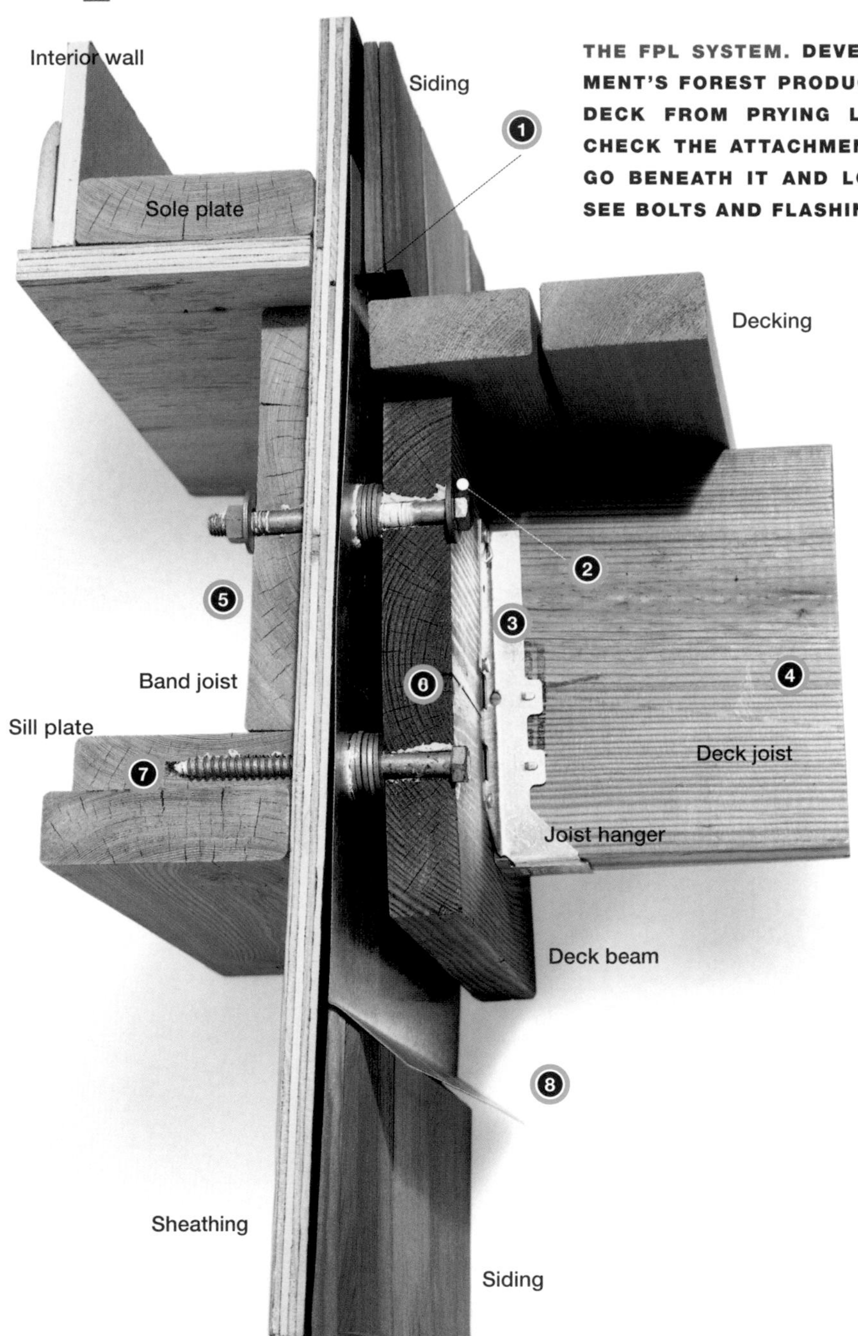

THE FPL SYSTEM. DEVELOPED BY RESEARCHERS AT THE U.S. GOVERNMENT'S FOREST PRODUCTS LABORATORY, THIS APPROACH WILL KEEP A DECK FROM PRYING LOOSE—AND IT WILL HELP PREVENT ROT. TO CHECK THE ATTACHMENT BETWEEN A HOUSE AND AN EXISTING DECK, GO BENEATH IT AND LOOK AT THE MAIN CONNECTION. IF YOU DON'T SEE BOLTS AND FLASHING, THEY'RE PROBABLY NOT THERE.

1. Tuck flashing under exterior siding. Use galvanized flashing, because copper-laden runoff from pressure-treated wood (see page 136) will corrode aluminum over time.

2. Use ½-inch-diameter bolts with nuts and washers wherever possible, for extra strength. Insert two to four washers as spacers so the deck beam can dry out.

3. Attach metal hanger with nails specified by the hanger's manufacturer. To avoid penetrating flashing with long nails, either attach the hangers and hammer over the nail tips before bolting the deck beam to the house, or switch to short, thick fasteners called hanger nails and reduce the load on each hanger as directed by the manufacturer.

4. Use pressure-treated lumber for beams and joists. Shown is an arsenic-free type.

5. If the band joist is not securely attached to the structural framing of the house, strengthen the connection before installing the deck beam. Hammer 16d nails at an angle so they penetrate through the sheathing into both the band joist and either the sole or sill plate. Space these nails every 8 inches.

6. After installing flashing, temporarily hang the deck beam in order to drill bolt holes. Then remove the beam, squirt caulk in the holes, and immediately reposition the beam in order to tighten the bolts.

7. Where access on both sides of the wall is limited, a ½-inch-diameter lag bolt may be used. It must reach at least 1½ inches into solid wood, such as the band joist, the sill, or studs. If the sill rests on the foundation, use expanding anchor bolts.

8. Extend the sheet of flashing below deck beam and bend the lip out over siding.

TOM SILVA'S SYSTEM: ADDING A DECK TO A HOUSE IN LEXINGTON, MASSACHUSETTS, *THIS OLD HOUSE* CONTRACTOR TOM SILVA PAYS PARTICULAR ATTENTION TO THE BEAM THAT CONNECTS THE DECK TO THE HOUSE AND CARRIES ALL THE SUPPORTING JOISTS. "IT'S WHERE 99 PERCENT OF MISTAKES ARE MADE," HE SAYS. THESE ARE THE KIND OF MISTAKES THAT HAVE CATASTROPHIC RESULTS.

TECHNIQUES

1 Preparing the job: Because a beam pressed tight against a house can trap moisture and encourage rot, Tom created a gap for air using spacers shaped to fit the recessed foundation of the house. He cut the spacers from scraps of pressure-treated wood, nailed them on and then drilled two holes through each spacer and the beam, one hole near the top edge, another at the bottom.

2 Placing the beam: Tom and his nephew Charlie Silva jockeyed the beam into position. Aiming through the top holes previously made, they drilled into the house's wooden sill and screwed in lag bolts. Through the lower holes, they installed masonry anchor bolts into the concrete foundation.

3 Defending against water: For flashing, Tom used an adhesive-backed flexible membrane made of polyethylene film and rubberized asphalt. He prefers it to metal flashing because it makes a watertight seal around any fasteners that penetrate it. Because the material could degrade in ultraviolet light, however, he makes sure to cover it with siding and decking. To prevent rot, Tom constructs the entire deck frame from pressure-treated wood. For the decking, Tom sometimes uses cedar or redwood, or a Brazilian hardwood called ipe. (For more on rot-resistant woods, see page 130.)

[hands on deck]

The sticky black material self-seals around nails and bolts, something no metal can do. But it degrades in sunlight, so the crew covered it with siding.

Tom also made sure the deck slopes slightly away from the family room. "Slanting it by even half a bubble will do the job," he says, referring to the marks on the level's vial. "It's supposed to be standard practice, but you'd be surprised at how many new decks are completely level."

paint and *varnish won't last on a deck, but a penetrating oil (with mildewicide) rolled on every spring and fall will preserve the wood's natural looks and keep the gray at bay.*

After building the deck's sturdy supporting framework—pressure-treated 2x10 joists and 6x6 posts anchored with metal brackets into concrete pilings—Tom laid down deck boards made of ipe ("*EE-pay*"), a durable Brazilian hardwood (for more on ipe, see page 134). Instead of face-nailing all the boards, Tom glued them down with waterproof polyurethane adhesive and used a few 8d stainless-steel nails, shot with a nail gun, to hold boards in place while the glue set.

THE CRITICAL CONNECTION

But the key to proper deck installation isn't the decking itself—it's how the deck is attached to the house. Home-owner Betty Gerisch knows that only too well. One evening, she was nudging through a dinner-party crowd, aiming for a buffet table on the deck of an Atlanta house. Suddenly, she heard a loud *crack* and found herself falling through the air. The deck had pulled away from the side of the house and collapsed, dumping 60 guests onto a concrete patio 18 feet below and scalding dozens of them in a torrent of overturned grills and chafing dishes. Ambulances jammed the street as rescue workers helped people with broken bones and third-degree burns. "In one instant, life can change dramatically," she says. "And all because of a badly built deck."

Decks are phenomenally popular in the United States, yet structural defects are common. Moreover, deck collapses tend to occur just when the potential for injury is greatest: when a crowd gathers. But a deck can handle the rowdiest gang of fraternity brothers as long as the beam (or ledger) that carries the floor joists is properly connected to the side of the house. Robert Falk, a structural engineer with the U.S. Forest Products Laboratory in Madison, Wisconsin, looked into the problem of deck failures after hearing of a deck-related death. Using a database to search five years of newspaper articles from around the country, he found that nearly every collapsed deck had been attached with nails, rather than bolts, and that investigators had pinpointed the nails as the cause of collapse. As people gather on a deck, their weight and movement translate not just into a downward force but also into an outward force that acts as a lever prying the

« In one instant, life can change dramatically," she says. "And all because of a badly built deck. »

[handsondeck]

When the deck on this house collapsed during a party in 1992, it killed a woman. Building officials found that the lag bolts had penetrated only the sheathing of the house—they were not anchored into anything solid.

deck away from the house. Nails resist the downward force but are no match for the outward force. Held in place only by friction, nails tend to loosen when wood alternately shrinks and swells with changes in moisture content and temperature. In contrast, a lag bolt, which looks like a giant screw, has as much as nine times the pullout resistance of a nail for every inch of penetration, Falk says.

Better still is the metal-to-metal connection of a true bolt fitted with a nut on the other side. Placing a washer on both sides spreads the pulling force over a larger portion of the beam. "You'd rip the whole structure apart before those bolts would pull out," Falk says. Both of these connectors offer an extra benefit over nails: They don't suddenly pull out. If the deck is inspected annually, early signs of loosening will show up as a widening gap against the house.

Concrete columns provide rot-proof support for decks and other outdoor structures. Making a column usually requires two pours: first to create the wide, mushroom-shaped footing upon which it rests, then to make the column itself. But Tom uses broad plastic pans to make the job easier. Slipped onto a standard fiberboard column form, the pans allow both footing and column to be made with just one pour.

[shading outdoor spaces]

IN WINTER, FEW THINGS FEEL COZIER THAN A ROOM FILLED WITH the warmth of the sun. Yet in summer the great orb turns from friend to foe, relentlessly pouring heat through windows, and turning decks and patios into outdoor frying pans. "A shadeless house can be a misery," says architect Robert A.M. Stern. A shade structure, however, can be an architectural asset.

when shaded *by a porch or pergola, a house not only gains an outdoor shelter; it also gains protection from summer sun that can heat up interior rooms and boost energy costs.*

Before the advent of central air-conditioning, the need to block the summer sun greatly influenced house design, as architects routinely incorporated porches and wide roof overhangs. "Fortunately," says Stern, "we are again discovering that we can do better than simply sticking an umbrella into a picnic table." As in the past, the simplest way to make some shade is by adding awnings, which were ubiquitous on American houses before World War II. "I can't imagine a style of house they don't work with," says Stern, who frequently adds manually or electrically operated awnings to his designs. Larger stretches of fabric can also be suspended horizontally over patios and decks, providing instant relief—especially in a yard that has no trees. In addition to the shade, Stern likes the

Top: The pergola at Dick Silva's house (page 149) is an elegant affair built with straightforward techniques. From start to finish, construction took 1½ days. Tom Silva screwed the rafters to a ledger board so he could lift them all into place at one time. Bottom: After resting the outer ends of the rafters on two redwood headers nailed to 6x6 posts, Tom and Dick screwed the ledger to the house over bitumen waterproofing strips. To further shield the joint, Tom fitted lead-coated copper flashing over the ledger.

Cooler and more open than a covered porch, a vine-covered pergola creates a shady haven for outdoor living. The simple structure shown here supports fruit-laden grapevines over a patio in California's Napa Valley.

[shading outdoor spaces]

Not all shade-makers are built-in. A simple cloth canopy held up with metal poles, for instance, provides plenty of cover, yet it can be quickly disassembled and stored at the end of the day. The holes in the fabric vent hot air and provide glimpses of the sky.

"incredible festiveness" that colorful awnings give to a house, a feeling he compares to the billowing sails of a tall ship. Although awnings need washing and periodic repair, the maintenance is minimal compared to the payoff in service and style. "They give a wonderful sense of the seasons," says Stern.

Another architectural element that's making a comeback is the pergola, which also integrates well with any style of architecture. A relatively simple structure, a pergola (derived from a Latin word meaning "projecting roof") consists of horizontal boards or trelliswork supported by classic columns, plain posts, or even metal poles. "Since the pergola extends from the house, it's a transitional element that's not wholly dependent on the house's style," says Stern. "You can have whatever you want." The shade comes from leafy vines planted at the column bases and allowed to climb up and spread over the top. Instead of vines, the structure sometimes has a canvas cover that is pulled back and forth across the top. "You can have lunch out there in the middle of the day and then pull it back in the evening," says Stern.

The covered porch—perhaps the most familiar, and American, of all shade-makers—has long kept the sun from scorching homeowners. But while putting a roof onto the side of a house can solve a problem, it also sometimes creates one. Earlier this century, architects became too casual about where they placed porches, says Stern, with the result that many living and dining rooms were kept in perpetual, sunless gloom. "A porch shouldn't be placed where it makes so much shade that a room behind it is darkened," he adds. "That's a big reason why people stopped liking porches in the first place." Yet the right porch is a wonderful amenity. It should be roomy—no less than 15 feet deep, says Stern, to make a space that's big enough for a sofa and some chairs, or a big table where people can gather on a summer's evening. "Just be careful where you site it," says Stern. "Unlike an awning, you won't be able to roll it up and stow it away at the end of the season."

Wisteria

Bougainvillea

Honeysuckle

Grape

Wisteria (*Fabaceae*). **In most climates, a fast grower that produces fragrant, hanging clusters of violet, white, or blue flowers.** Bougainvillea (*Bougainvilla glabra*). **A thorny climber that thrives in warm climates, where it typically blooms year-round.** Honeysuckle (*Lonicera*). **Produces sweet-smelling white, yellow, pink, purple, coral, rose, or red flowers; thrives most places.** Grape (*Vitis*). **Needs plenty of sun, but quickly forms a dense leaf mat in most climates; many varieties yield edible grapes.**

A LUSH CANOPY OF TWINING TENDRILS, VERDANT FOLIAGE, AND SWEET-SMELLING BLOSSOMS COMPLETES A PERGOLA'S MISSION. PLANTED AT THE BASE OF EACH COLUMN AND GIVEN OCCASIONAL DOSES OF FERTILIZER AND COMPOST, A FLOWERING VINE WILL SPREAD OVER THE STRUCTURE IN TWO TO FIVE YEARS, DEPENDING ON THE CLIMATE. AND THERE ARE DOZENS OF VARIETIES TO CHOOSE FROM, ALSO DEPENDING ON YOUR CLIMATE. NO MATTER WHAT THE WEATHER, SUNLIGHT LEVELS, AND SOIL TYPE IN YOUR AREA, THERE ARE PLENTY OF CLIMBERS THAT WILL PROVIDE THE FOLIAGE AND FLOWERS YOU'D MOST LIKE BETWEEN YOU AND THE SUN. THE ONES ABOVE ARE SOME POPULAR CHOICES.

fine vines

"YOU don't know for CERTAIN HOW THINGS WILL TURN OUT UNTIL BRICK comes out of the KILN."

[concrete and cement]

IN THE YEARS PRIOR TO WORLD WAR II, MOST ANYONE WHO wanted just a smidgen of concrete to patch a sidewalk, fill a hole, or anchor a fence post had to cadge leftover slurry from job sites. The only other options were to have some delivered (minimum order: two tons) or hire a contractor and his big drum mixer to whip up a batch. Then along came Arthur Avril. As the owner of an Akron, Ohio company that delivered concrete by truck, he'd seen plenty of scavengers carry away his surplus in buckets, wheelbarrows, even ashpans. So, in 1936, he started shoveling dry cement, sand and gravel into paper sacks. His nephew, Jack Avril, remembers the first bagged concrete: "I was 5 when all this was happening. He just said one day, 'Why don't we put this up without water, like Duncan Hines cake mix?'"

An alternative to standard cement deliveries, some companies use trucks that mix ingredients on site. This eliminates waste—and a lot of anxiety.

The elder Avril's epiphany, which he dubbed Sakrete, made concrete available to the masses, and the masses made his product's name synonymous with bagged concrete. Now, scores of companies offer bags of dry mix, which, on an average day, rumble out of home centers and lumber yards by the thousands, destined for patios, walkways and deck footings across the land. But in addition to the basic gray all-purpose concrete Avril would have recognized, home-owners can now choose from bags or buckets of patching mixes, topping mixes, and masonry mixes, not to mention mixes for anchoring bolts, coating walls, laying bricks and leveling floors. Some mixes are strengthened with crack-stopping fiberglass; others have adhesion-enhancing vinyl additives. Still others require no mixing at all: Just dig a hole and pour it in.

All these blends have one ingredient in common: Portland cement—a fine, flourlike powder that gives concrete its color and rock-hard strength. Natural cement—as opposed to the manufactured, Portland variety—was discovered by the Romans, who mined it from pumice deposits on the slopes of Mount Vesuvius and elsewhere. Mixed with water, the crushed pumice turned, as if under Medusa's gaze, to stone. Today, instead of relying on volcanoes, manufacturers bake the necessary minerals (calcium, silicon, aluminum and iron) in giant rotating kilns heated to a super-Vesuvian 2,800 degrees Fahrenheit. Roman builders found they could stretch their

Mixing it up. When the job is small enough for bag mix, Tom follows some simple mixing rules. He stirs the dry mix in a wheelbarrow or bin, to blend the gravel that settles in shipping. Then, into a little crater in the middle of the mix, he adds some clean water, which he chops in thoroughly with a hoe or shovel. "You want to add the water slowly, in stages, as you mix," he says. After a few minutes of churning, the wet concrete should be uniformly stiff—like peanut butter—with no dry spots. Tom adds a bit more water if the concrete is crumbly; if it's slightly soupy, he'll put in more dry mix.

[concrete and cement]

precious supply of cement—and make it even stronger—by adding crushed stone, gravel and sand. Presto! The world's first concrete. Today's mix isn't much different. A typical bag of the basic mix contains one part cement, 2 to 3 parts sand, and 3 to 5 parts gravel or rock. "It's fantastic for a step or a patch," says Tom Silva, "but I wouldn't go past a dozen or so bags." Because each 60-pound bag yields only 1 cubic foot of concrete, it's too much effort and too expensive to use on big jobs. And using too many small batches also raises the risk of cold joints—weak spots that result when one batch starts to set before the next one is poured.

Stirring concrete is hard work. "If you aren't breaking a sweat, then you aren't mixing it right," Tom says. To ease the task, many people add a lot of extra water to the mix, creating a stirrable soup. The waterlogged concrete, however, just ends up weaker and more susceptible to shrinking, cracking and abrasion. Once water is added to a dry mix, the clock starts ticking. A basic mix sets in about 90 minutes, depending on the weather. Heat speeds the process, and cold slows it down, but job-site Betty Crockers can tamper with the process by adding a manufactured set-retardant when temperatures soar, or an accelerator when they plunge. But sometimes even the most careful work comes to naught. More than once, Tom says, "We've finished smoothing out a sidewalk when a dog comes up, wagging his tail, and walks right through it." No wonder sidewalk masons zealously guard their handiwork as long as they can.

Once set, fresh concrete needs to rest for six to eight days under moist, frost-protected conditions so that the cement and water molecules can bond and gain strength. Swaddling new work in damp burlap or

ANCHOR CEMENT: Used indoors or out to anchor bolts, railings, and hooks. Sets in less than 10 minutes. Expands slightly.

FAST-SETTING: Just pour water in a hole, brace a post upright, and dump the mix in. Sets in 20-40 min.

SAND MIX: Resurfaces and patches chipped concrete. Should be used in thicknesses less than 2 inches.

Brighten up your gray. **Custom colors have broadened the concrete palette beyond dull gray. Most color additives, which come either as powders or liquids, are thrown onto into the water before mixing with concrete. A new type of brush-on dye gives old surfaces a different tint. Still another approach is to sprinkle powdered colorant over the slab just before troweling begins. This saves money—colorant is expensive—because only the surface of the slab is colored, not the entire thickness.**

MORTAR MIX: A blend of cement, ground limestone and graded sand makes a mix for laying brick and setting stone.

HIGH EARLY STRENGTH: Gains strength very quickly. This fast-setting mix is especially useful in cold weather.

RESURFACING: Brushed or troweled in ½-inch layers over old concrete, it makes surfaces look new. Additives strengthen the bond.

BASIC MIX: Standard mix is economical but has long setting time. Should be poured in a layer at least 2 inches thick.

COLORED: Adobe-colored concrete cures to a warm, earthy hue that is not created by synthetic pigments.

REINFORCED: Contains tiny synthetic fibers that increase tensile strength and reduce cracking. Eliminates need for wire reinforcement in sidewalks and driveways.

plastic sheets helps ensure a complete cure. Properly mixed and cared for, concrete will stiffen enough to walk on in a day or so, but will take 28 days to reach most of its compressive strength—at least 2,000 pounds per square inch. After that, hardening will proceed—slowly—as the cement continues reacting to trace amounts of water. There's no turning back, except via jackhammer.

A DELIVERY ALTERNATIVE

There is nothing quite like the approaching growl of a loaded concrete mixer for quickening the pulse and bringing a cold sweat to the brow. Anyone who's ordered truck-delivered concrete has probably agonized about how much to ask for. Too much wastes money; too little can ruin a project. For a more relaxed approach, one option is to call a company with trucks that keep ingredients separate during transit. Though not yet common, onsite mixing ensures fresher concrete and more working time before it sets. The truck mixes just the amount that's needed. And the trucks are smaller than standard mixers, so they can get into backyards. Search the *Yellow Pages* for suppliers with "mobile mix" or "short pour" services.

hydraulic
cement expands to plug holes even where water is present, making it ideal for emergency repairs to leaking foundations.

[a perfect pathway]

A POWER SHOVEL'S BUCKET SCRAPES THE CRUMBLY 60-FOOT headwall of Shanesville pit, mine No. 4, dislodging an avalanche of shale fragments. "We have the glaciers to thank for all this," says Lauren Gonser, a manager at the Belden Brick Company. "The glaciers scraped the soils off Canada and deposited them right here," he adds, noting the surrounding hills.

The particular look of a brick pathway depends on the color and shape of the brick itself, as well as the pattern in which it is layed (above). Grain and color are affected by the blend of clays and minerals and their firing in the kiln. A facing brick is made to be seen, and often has a textured or specially colored surface. Building brick, on the other hand, sometimes called common brick, has no special texture or color. Paving brick is an abrasion-resistant, low-absorption material ideally suited to use in streets and walkways. At right, Norm inspects 200-year-old brick as Roger Cook looks on. The brick were salvaged from a building in Boston's Scully Square.

For 110 years, Belden Brick in Sugar Creek, Ohio, has been mining or "winning" clay and shale from pits in eastern Ohio. Each year, Belden can produce 220 million brick—one of the oldest and most durable of manmade building materials.

The scree left at the base of the headwall may appear to be so much rock, but to the ceramic engineer in charge of brick-making, it's composed of distinctly different minerals that ultimately determine the appearance and performance of the brick. One pit can yield very different kinds of clays. At mine No. 4, the headwall actually has numbers pinned to it so the shovel operator can dig out the desired ingredients.

The next step is to pulverize the rock into gritty dust. Trucks arriving at plant No. 8, one of Belden's six brick-making facilities, dump their loads into the crusher, where giant steel teeth grind the rock into small lumps. A series of conveyor belts ferry this detritus to the grinder, where a pair of 7-ton muller wheels crush the lumps, much the way millstones grind wheat into flour. Particles small enough

[a perfect pathway]

to pass through three layers of vibrating 14-mesh screen are deposited in holding bins. Belden quarries two basic materials: a whitish fireclay and a soft brown shale. Each type is kept separate so they can be mixed in precise proportions to produce brick of a particular color. From the holding bins, this clay "flour" travels to the pug mill, where it is blended or "tempered" with water and made into brick.

Before 1863, nearly all brick was molded,

TECHNIQUES

1 Water and ice are the enemies of brick, so *This Old House* landscaper Roger Cook only uses brick rated SW (severe weathering). For this project, water-struck bricks that look handmade were mixed with antique bricks.

2 Before the path is dug, 1x2 stakes are driven into the ground to mark the borders. Spruce 1x3 boards will be fastened to the stakes with drywall screws to define the exact edges of the 48-inch-wide walkway.

3 One secret of a stable walkway is to remove all soil containing organic material. Cook advises digging down 2 feet when in doubt.

4 "To keep the walk from walking on you," Cook says, the bed under the brick must be filled with gravel—5 tons of it for this 42-foot path.

5 The spruce boards that control the sides and width of the walkway are bent into curves by kerfing them—sawing partway through across the board every half inch or so. Boards should be securely placed so the width of the walk varies by less than ¼ inch.

6 As he defines the edges with a soldier course (bricks bedded vertically with wide faces touching), Cook is careful to frequently check the cross-pitch. This 4-foot walk is sloped ⅛ inch per foot to the left so that water will drain off the top rather than pool on the surface.

7 Another secret: Stone dust, available from quarries, is the essential ingredient of great brick walkways because it compacts much better than sand. Roger uses 2 inches of it above the gravel underlayment, tamps it with a machine, and keeps it moist while laying brick. To control the level of the final surface, he makes a screed, cut from a 2x4, that he uses to scrape the surface just before he places the bricks. The screed is cut to fit precisely between the soldier courses.

8 Each and every brick is firmly tamped to set it into the stone dust below. The novice pathway-maker often skips this time-consuming and tedious step, but does so at the risk of leaving in the walk wobbly bricks that will eventually shift. A shifted brick is more than an eyesore—it's a tripping hazard. Brick scars easily, so a dead-blow rubber mallet is a better choice than a metal hammer.

5

6

7

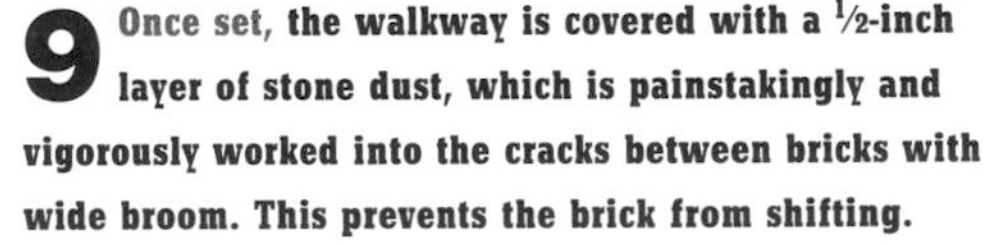

9 Once set, the walkway is covered with a ½-inch layer of stone dust, which is painstakingly and vigorously worked into the cracks between bricks with a wide broom. This prevents the brick from shifting.

10 Finally, the completed pathway gets a long washdown with a hose. The water will help settle the underlayment and set the bricks in the stone dust. The spruce side boards should be left in place for a week or longer while the bricks adjust to the weight of people walking on them.

8

9

10

[a perfect pathway]

using "soft-mud" clay with a 20 to 30 percent moisture content. Then Cyrus Chambers Jr. invented the first commercially successful machine to extrude a continuous bar of "stiff-mud" clay (12 to 15 percent moisture content), like a noodle out of a pasta maker. The process is much the same for modern brick. Subjected to 1,000 pounds per square inch of pressure, the clay exits the extruder as a smooth column which is methodically sliced into "green" brick by banks of taut stainless-steel wire. Workers then stack the brick into "chimneys" atop rolling cars for the trip through a 530-foot long tunnel kiln (pronounced "kill"). Kiln cars laden with green brick roll from one end of the kiln to the other through the gas-fueled firing zone—what Gonser calls "hell for brick."

For eight hours, the brick are subjected to temperatures as high as 2,100 degrees Fahrenheit. This draws out all the water, then partially liquefies or "vitrifies" the clay. The brick are then moved away from the heat so they won't melt into distorted "clinkers." Getting everything right—the blend of clays, the amount of water, and the firing temperature and time—is the brick-maker's biggest anxiety. "You don't know for certain how things will turn out until brick comes out of the kiln," says Robert Belden, great-grandson of the company's founder. "And at that point, it's too late to do anything."

Belden also operates several beehive kilns that produce specialty brick. These kilns give the brick-maker the greatest control. The fireman can increase the time in the kiln to get low-absorption industrial brick, or add coal, zinc or manganese to the kiln to modify the brick's color. But because it takes about 30 days to load, fire, cool, and unload a beehive kiln, brick fired in this way are more costly to make than those from a continuous kiln.

Even after firing, there is one final step: blending. Fired brick varies widely in color depending on its composition, its position in the kiln and the amount of heat it's subjected to. To make sure whatever is built with the brick has a uniform shade overall and doesn't look patchy, the brick stacks are taken apart by hand, randomly sorted by machine, then restacked into 525-brick cubes for shipping.

custom-fit brick

A PATHWAY WITH CURVES OR ANGLES USUALLY CALLS FOR BRICKS THAT ARE CUT TO FIT. BRICKS CAN BE CHIPPED TO SHAPE WITH A MASON'S HAMMER (TOP RIGHT), OR THEY CAN BE PLACED ON A BED OF STONE DUST AND WHACKED WITH A HAMMER AND A VERY WIDE COLD CHISEL. BUT NOTHING WILL CUT AS NICELY AS A MASONRY WET SAW (BOTTOM RIGHT). THE SAW IS FITTED WITH A DIAMOND-GRIT BLADE COOLED BY A SPRAY OF WATER. THE SOUND OF A STEEL BLADE SPINNING AGAINST BRICK IS REMINISCENT OF A FINGERNAIL SCRAPED AGAINST BLACKBOARD, BUT THE RESULTS ARE REMARKABLY SATISFYING. WHETHER IT'S WORTH RENTING ONE, ROGER SAYS, "DEPENDS ON HOW NEAT YOU WANT TO BE."

BASKET WEAVE.
Deep vertical soldiers on the sides help stabilize this ageless design. The pattern works only for bricks that are half as wide as they are long. (Most bricks are 4 by 8 inches).

DIAGONAL.
A traditional pattern twisted to the diagonal is edged with bricks laid flat, called a stretcher course. The design requires a significant amount of custom cutting.

COLONIAL WILLIAMSBURG.
This pattern is narrow (about 36 to 40 inches using standard pavers), but it accommodates varying sizes of bricks because the rows are not linked to each other.

MODIFIED BASKET WEAVE.
A simple basket-weave can gain visual depth with the use of bricks of sharply contrasting colors. The design is difficult to work with in a pathway that curves.

SPANISH BOND.
This motif uses four bricks, each twice as long as it is wide, to trap a half brick in the center. The design is simpler to put down than it looks but does not curve easily.

HERRINGBONE.
Herringbone themes are popular in brickwork, but require a lot of brick cutting at the edges. The edges of this path, for example, need a half brick every foot.

ANGLED BASKET WEAVE.
A basket-weave turned 45 degrees and edged with two rows of bricks laid on their side, called a rowlock stretcher course, lines streets in at least one Maryland town.

RUNNING BOND.
In this style, the space between two bricks falls in the middle of adjacent bricks. Shifting the joint to fall in the first third or fourth of neighboring bricks changes the look entirely.

NEW OLD BRICK

Using age-old techniques, Belden also makes hand-molded brick for restoration projects. First, a mold from the hundreds in inventory is selected. The molder takes a wad of soft clay and bounces it on a sand-covered table to form a "slug," then a thrower lifts the 8-pound slug overhead and heaves it into the mold. He presses the clay into the corners and uses a wire "strike" to remove excess. Finally he shakes the mold and inverts it to pop out the green brick. A four-person molding crew (one washer, one molder, two throwers) can produce about 100 brick per hour.

[building stone walls]

A STONEMASON HAS POWERFUL INCENTIVE TO DO GOOD WORK. Even a second-rate wall may last 50 years, and a careless mason could spend a lifetime averting his eyes from a botched job. Nor would he forget whose mess it was. "Everybody's work is different," says Rico D'Eramo, who laid his first stone in Italy at the age of 10. "You hear a voice, you know it's Pavarotti." So D'Eramo and his sons, Vincent and Robert, are taking their usual care with yet another wall, tucking each stone into its bed of mortar so it will sleep there for a century. It is a low, double-faced patio wall with just enough mortar to hold it straight and strong. Using too much mortar is like cheating, Robert says, and detracts from the natural look.

wedges
made of brick scraps absorb moisture from fresh mortar, preventing it from staining the stone's face.

A novice admiring a stone wall may not consciously understand why he finds it beautiful. But a mason like Rico D'Eramo knows, having trained his eye, mind and hand with literally tons of experience. Driving past a wall, he sizes it up in a flash, noting the relationship of each stone to its neighbors, the neatness and consistency of the joints and the artful use of mortar to stitch the stones together. Then he calls out his verdict—"This is a good wall" or "This wall is painful on my eyes." But when a wall has been done right—well, D'Eramo puts finger and thumb together and flips them open in the quintessential Italian gesture of love.

The D'Eramos, father and sons, travel together. They arrive at the site with their tools, a truckload of select Connecticut fieldstone (mostly soft granite), a wheelbarrow, and a muscular helper to mix mortar. From the truck emerges one more necessity—bowls of fresh peaches, grapes and figs to snack on in the sunshine.

They sort the stones carefully. Those with flat surfaces, pleasing grain, and 90-degree angles go into special piles. These are reserved for positions of honor in the top and corners of the wall. Inferior chunks get tossed in a heap. They will fill the wall's interior and never see daylight again. Then, gloveless and with only

With hammer and chisel, Rico D'Eramo dresses a stone before setting it into the base of a wall. "Some stones obey you, some don't listen," he says. Using such aphorisms and the example of his 65 years in the trade, D'Eramo has taught stonemasonry to his sons, Vincent and Robert. The three men know that a wall of substance will last longer than its builders.

[building stone walls]

sneakers to protect their toes, the D'Eramos go to work. They dig a trench, build a foundation and begin laying stone. They joke and banter and argue. "Working is good for you physically, mentally—and financially," says Rico with a grin. The sons roll their eyes and call out a few gentle insults. But all the while, the wall grows taller.

Stones differ by region and type, ranging from the hard granites of New England to the

TECHNIQUES

1 Even a low wall **must be set on a sturdy foundation to keep it from toppling due to frost heave and soil movement. This one rests on a 3-foot-deep base of crushed masonry stone topped with steel-reinforced concrete. The first course of stones is set into the wet concrete.**

2 The 15-inch space **between the wall faces is filled with rubble. Masons think before they lift; even so, many stones are handled six times before finding a home.**

3 A mason **staggers stones so that joints never form a straight line or cross. Some longer stones are turned inward, extending through the wall to add strength.**

4 This will be a wall to sit on, so keeping it level is important. The D'Eramos do this by setting stakes at either end and at the center of the wall, then running string between the stakes at a height of 23 inches.

5 Some masons put all the large stones near the bottom of a wall so they won't have to lift them. The D'Eramos prefer a more random look. If they split a large stone, they never put the halves where both can be seen together. Instead, they save one for the other side.

6 Good masons use stone economically. "The old Italians are like the old Yankees," Robert D'Eramo says. "Everything gets used. They never leave even a pebble on the site."

7 Even when using mortar, a good mason tries to fit stones carefully so the wall looks as natural as possible. The D'Eramos rake excess mortar from exterior joints of the partially dry wall using a simple tool: a stick.

subtle sandstones of the Midwest to the fossil-bearing limestones of the Florida Keys. Rico taught his sons about local stone in the order he learned: first to haul water, then to mix mortar, rake joints, break stones, build the back of a wall, and then the front. Finally, they were allowed to weave the top and corners.

Vincent drops a stone with a mutter. "*Fascia brutta*," he says. Ugly face. Robert

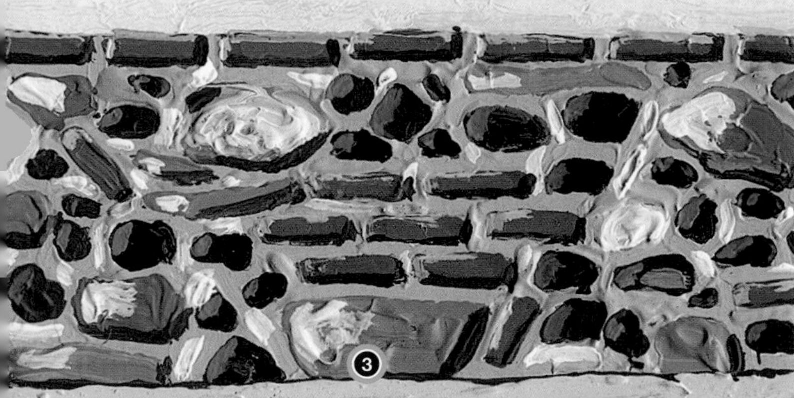

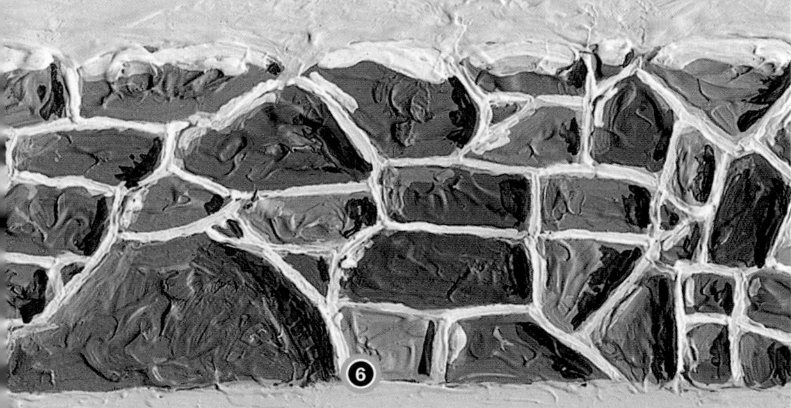

knocks a wobble knob off one stone, then neatly splits another. He scoops up mortar with his trowel and sets a stone in place. "You take pictures of the wall in your mind," Rico says. "Then you go find the stones that fit." And how to judge the results? "There's no reason to build a wall unless you want it to last forever," says Robert.

Late in the afternoon, Rico pauses, beckons and holds up his aging trowel, its steel blade stone-ground to half the length of the ones Robert and Vincent are using. Next to the worn trowel, he holds up his hand, the stubby fingers strong and whole. He nods from one to the other. Steel wears out, he

***

STONES DIFFER BY REGION AND type, and so walls vary, too. The drawings illustrate eight of the most common types.

1. Dry-stack boundary. **This mortar-less wall creates a lot line with whatever stone is at hand. A boundary wall is usually rough, without a cap or top line of carefully chosen stone. It can range from a glorified rock pile to a highly refined creation, depending on the skill of the mason. A finished boundary wall has a flatter, more carefully selected top course of stones for a cleaner look. A double-faced boundary wall is two or even three stones thick, with a face on either side. In any dry-stack wall, some annual movement—and thus some annual maintenance—can be expected.**

2. Dressed. **This wall, also known as an ashlar wall, is built of shaped or cut stone, carefully joined for a refined appearance. It is a labor-intensive and therefore expensive style, requiring great skill. In this example, the stones to the right of center have not been staggered carefully; they create a weak joint running from top to bottom.**

3. Knapped flint. **The beauty of this wall is its hodgepodge of materials. The primary ingredient is flint stone, a particularly hard type of quartz, which is split and set in mortar. Brick, tile and other types of stone, often large boulders, are also incorporated and set at odd angles.**

4. Semidry. **Also known as a dry-look wall, this type uses mortar to stitch stones together from the inside or back. Surface mortar is scratched away for a natural appearance, as if the stones were merely stacked. It is a permanent wall that should never need maintenance. The double-faced version has two outer faces and an interior filled with rubble, like the low wall on the previous pages. Because water can drain from the interior voids through channels called weep holes, winter ice should not crack or explode the wall. For stability, the wall must be built on a foundation deep enough to reach below the frost line.**

5. Pennsylvania flat-stone. **A low, semidry wall made of fieldstone (also called a New York flat-stone wall). Natural looking, it can be the most expensive of all to construct because small stones require much effort to cement together. The stones are common in Pennsylvania and New York, but not elsewhere.**

6. Wet. **A carefully made wall in which stones are cut and fitted with exposed mortar and consistent spacing. Many fireplaces are built this way. The weight of big stones tends to force out the mortar, so they are sometimes stabilized by masonry wedges (the D'Eramos use bits of brick). A wet wall can be built of various stones, but through-wall drainage must be provided. Often, a wet wall's mortar is dark in color and recessed slightly to create interesting shadow patterns and emphasize the stones. As a rule, this type of wall has a contrived appearance and should not be built where a natural-looking wall is desired.**

7. Semidry retaining. **Because it supports a soil embankment, only one side of this wall is visible. To improve drainage, the soil side is often backfilled with gravel. For strength and aesthetics, the wall leans toward the embankment—about 1 inch per four feet of height.**

8. Boulder. **This is the least formal stone structure that can still be called a wall. Often used to mark a property line or erected purely for decoration, it is made of whatever large stones are available, rolled into a row. Vegetation eventually fills the gaps between boulders.**

[building stone walls]

seems to say, but the flesh never does. And he glances over at his two sons, at work building the wall.

USING CORAL IN THE LANDSCAPE

"I feel like a little kid building a fort," says stonemason Josh Billig. He's crouching in a pool of Miami sunshine at the foot of a rambling old Mediterranean-Revival mansion's stone stairway, chipping away at a hunk of coral rock with a loosely held hatchet. "I used to see old estates like this as a kid and think I'd have one someday." He chuckles at his early naïveté, fitting a stone into place. "Now I probably spend more time on estates by working in them than if I lived in one."

low walls *preserve views of the landscape beyond. Higher walls are better when the view must be concealed.*

Billig is repairing the damage Hurricane Andrew did to the 1922 Stone House at the historic Deering Estate. Few people can turn the cream-and-caramel-colored "coral rock" (which is actually a kind of limestone geologists call oolite) into artful, solid, lasting structures, and Billig is one of them. Black Bahamian craftsmen brought the technique to Florida decades ago, and some of the most charming houses in the area are built of coral rock. In the 1920s, workers beat the soft stone walls with chains and sprayed them with cow manure to make them look old and promote moss growth, thereby endowing them with instant pedigree.

On the Deering job, Billig, his installer Gregg Mulvihill, and their helpers finished rocking up two enormous three-story chimneys in which squared-off chunks of oolite form a tight-jointed pattern. Then they moved on to the stairs, where Billig uses keystone quarried in Key Largo that's been cut to reveal fossilized coral animals on its surface. On the wall beside the stairs, Billig is laying rough chunks of oolite veneer horizontally with wide, almost random joints, trying to match the house's original, haphazard workmanship.

"It's not very pretty, but it's historically accurate," he says with a shrug. "You have to discover the old technique and then try to match it." He looks pained—no proud stonemason likes a loose joint.

Using saws and grinders, Billig bullnosed (rounded-over) the keystone top of an umbrella table made of oolite. This is one piece of patio furniture that won't blow away.

« I feel like a little kid building a fort," says stonemason Josh Billig, chipping away with a hatchet. »

[landscaping with stone]

SOMEONE MUST HAVE LOVED THE waterfall in front of Bill and Joyce Duvall's house. But Roger Hopkins, the familiar stonemason from *This Old House*, winced each time he drove by. Nothing about the landscape made geologic sense. A mammoth, platter-shaped stone perched precariously atop smaller rocks, and water that seemed to come from nowhere cascaded into a pool surrounded by flat lawn and asphalt. Hopkins couldn't wait for a chance to fix it. Finally, he stopped by for a quick visit.

"The Japanese," says Hopkins (right), "use stone as the primary element of the landscape, with everything else—water and plants—wrapping around it. Then they create gardens by taking the elements of nature and arranging them into simplified, abstract landscapes. Not fussy or decorative, but scenic." Following these principles, Hopkins created the serene composition on the facing page.

In the brainstorming that followed, Bill Duvall brought out a picture of a garden with huge stones that he had admired during a trip to Japan. Without being too literal, the scene mimicked what nature might do, suggesting possibilities for the Duvalls' own oval of grass.

Vistas built with water and stone can be awesome, but placing stone just so is neither easy nor cheap. "Even in a small-scale garden, the stone has to be big—at least a ton," says Hopkins. "And it's got to be placed right. It has to look rooted, like it has seen the centuries pass by."

The Duvalls' property had plenty of boulders, unearthed when the house was built. But even after 40 years of exposure, they looked too fresh. So Hopkins prospected in the Duvalls' woods, pausing at every boulder. "I don't make any final decisions until I've seen many. It costs a lot to retrieve beautiful stone in the wild, so I give high marks to any I find lying near a road."

Hopkins eventually positioned several stones and bermed up the earth behind them, making the three-bay attached garage seem to disappear. The waterfall was rebuilt to look as if the water had actually cut through the granite stones. Above, he placed two mature Japanese cutleaf maples; their gnarly trunks look as though they've aged with the rocks. His final adjustment was to hide the asphalt driveway under a layer of pea gravel.

[patio and deck design]

ALMOST EVERYONE WANTS SOME SORT OF OUTDOOR LIVING SPACE near the house—a terrace, a deck, a patio, a pool area. Places for outdoor lounging and eating can make a house feel grand and permanent; without them, a house might seem like a bus stop. Unfortunately, the design of outdoor areas often falls through cracks between the architect's responsibility and that of the landscape designer. One designs the house, one designs the yard, and both ignore the link between the two. To avoid this, consider outdoor spaces at the very start of any project. Take a good look at the land around the house and remind yourself of what attracted you to it in the first place—don't just order up a raised deck and tack it on the back of the house.

provide *suitable drainage for a patio. The surface should slope slightly away from the house, even if water can drain through it.*

Consider a raised terrace or patio instead. Elevated on a bed of sand and gravel and supported with a short retaining wall, it should sit high enough to appear to float above the surrounding land, but not quite as high as the porch or entryway from which it extends. Such a patio offers an elegant, earthbound transition between the house and the grass. Of course, there's nothing wrong with trying the same approach using wood and decking materials; just keep the same principles in mind.

The grading and the landscaping around a deck or patio are as important as the structure itself. All too often, shrubbery is hauled in to mark the edges of a patio—an expensive proposition that tends to throw off the scale of the house and detract from the image of the house as commander of the landscape. A more effective—and usually cheaper—solution is to grade the site in a way that allows for interesting changes in contour and elevation. The patio can then stand on its own.

Another nettlesome spot is the steps leading out from the house. The typical approach—building two or three quick steps down—does nothing to unite the indoor and outdoor areas. Far better are steps containing a series of small landings that elongate the transition from one to the other, and make for a gentler passage.

No matter what the site, the key to a good inside-to-outside design is to respect all three parts of the property—the house, the transition space, and the land. The mistake most people make is to see them as separate and distinct from each other; the magic occurs when they are linked.

This patio is "stamped" concrete with a color wash—a cost-effective alternative to stone. The ground was banked at the front edge of the patio to eliminate the need for steps. The wood railing will be removed when inkberry shrubs grow tall enough to provide a visual barrier.

[building a patio]

LAY DOWN A DURABLE SURFACE, BLOT OUT THE MUD, AND civilization will follow. The Appian Way, a 350-mile road built with interlocking stone blocks, was the pride of the Roman Empire. These durable pavers withstood everything from the foot-slap of legions to the onslaught of wheels and weather. In fact, most of the ancient road is still intact, including a section of blocks laid in 312 B.C. at the Appian Gate in Rome. Distant cousin to such masonry masterwork is the patio, a suburban amenity like a short road linking house and landscape. In fact, the materials traditionally reserved for roads—stone, concrete, asphalt, even gravel—are increasingly used for patios, just as patio materials are landing in driveways. Anything is possible.

approximately *7.8 billion brick emerge from kilns in the United States every year, enough to build two Great Walls of China.*

Compared to deck construction, building a patio seems simple: There are no joist-span tables to consult, no beams to engineer. But before paving your paradise, check with local building officials—zoning regulations sometimes limit the amount of ground that can be covered by house and patios. Likewise, a patio should not cover part of a septic system or interrupt drainage swales.

Stone and brick can be mortared into place or rest atop compacted sand and gravel. In either case, patios should slope slightly away from the house. Poor soil conditions might even require a network of plastic drainage pipes beneath the gravel.

STONE

Local stone, whether New England granite, bluestone (right), or Pennsylvania slate, often suit the landscape best. Another reason for going with the local product: Shipping stone increases its cost considerably. Stone-setting techniques favor regionally appropriate solutions, too, being affected as much by the weather as by the availability of materials. Before choosing stone, think about how the patio will be used. Rough surfaces with irregular joints aren't kid-friendly or as suitable for entertaining as smooth surfaces.

BRICK

Grind shale into a fine "flour." Mix with water until plastic, then shape into a rectangle. Fire for eight hours at 2,100 degrees; let cool. Now you have a brick. When it comes to patios, brick is a traditional favorite. It has an earthy naturalness that beautifully complements green plants and bright flowers, and it's

The difference between a walk and a patio is sometimes delightfully difficult to determine, as this house near Madison, Wisconsin, shows. Blending the two into a single composition accentuates the landscape.

[building a patio]

relatively affordable. Salvaged brick cost a bit more than new, but it has a gentle, antique warmth that appeals to many people. Salvaged brick is suitable only in southern climes, however. Put on the ground up north, these soft, common bricks would disintegrate as water seeped inside and froze. "On the ground, you definitely want to use a hard paver brick," says Tom Silva. Paving bricks rated SW ("severe weathering") are fired longer and at higher temperatures than the face brick used to build walls. In Massachusetts, *This Old House* landscaping contractor Roger Cook usually digs down 8 to 12 inches, then installs a 3-to-4-inch blanket of gravel, topped with a setting bed of stone dust. "Stone dust packs firmer than sand," he says.

CONCRETE PAVERS

Although clay brick and natural stone share the paver market, the most popular choice is concrete, which comes in a surprisingly wide range of colors, shapes and sizes. Even better, concrete pavers are as sturdy as they are stylish. Because they're set in a bed of sand, pavers can move as the ground freezes and thaws, so

Brick is available in a wide variety of forms. Border brick (above) can be used as an accent at the edges of a patio or in the field. The raised buttons on this one can complement the flat surface of surrounding bricks. Crushed brick (far left) makes a lovely garden path and can be used for wider areas, but it crumbles to dust with wear. The material can be hard to find in some areas. Paver brick (left) is hard-fired, so it stands up well to traffic. Such brick is relatively uniform in shape, but irregularities in the surface make it susceptible to weather damage. Wood-molded brick (right) is made by machine but mimics the irregular shapes and textures of old handmade brick.

[building a patio]

installing concrete pavers

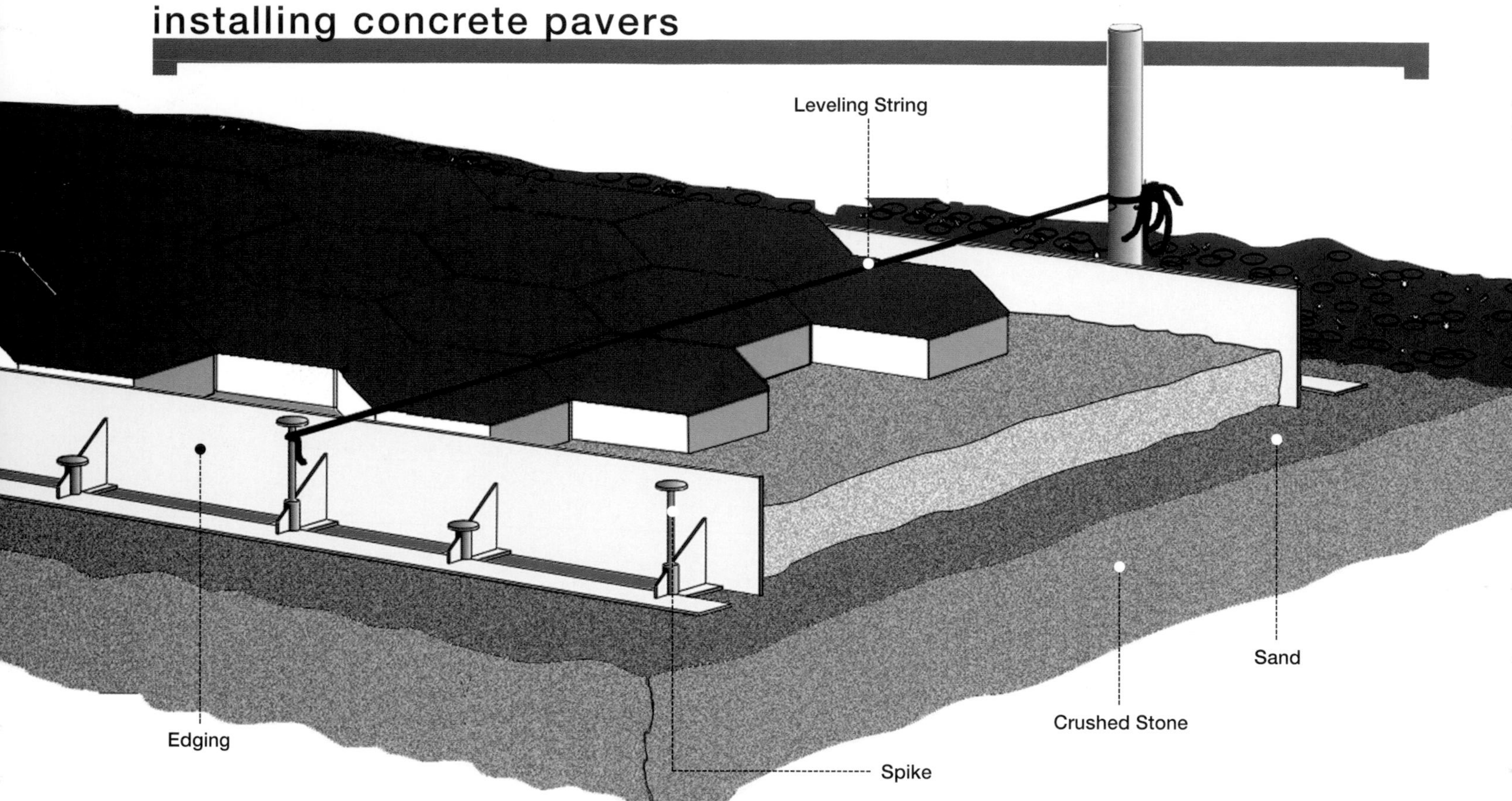

THE KEY TO BEAUTIFUL PAVERS IS BEAUTIFUL BEDDING. INCORRECTLY INSTALLED PAVERS CAN SHIFT OR POP OUT OF POSITION, RUINING THEIR LOOK AND PRESENTING A TRIPPING HAZARD. WITH A PROPER BASE, HOWEVER, THEY SHOULD REMAIN IN PLACE FOR DECADES. THE DRAWING ABOVE SHOWS A DRIVEWAY INSTALLATION; SIMILAR TECHNIQUES WOULD APPLY TO WALKS AND PATIOS, THOUGH THE LAYERS OF SAND AND STONE MAY NOT NEED TO BE QUITE AS THICK. FOR PATTERN IDEAS, SEE THE FACING PAGE.

A FOOT OR SO BELOW A CONCRETE PAVER DRIVE, SOIL SHOULD HAVE BEEN COMPACTED USING A FLAT-PLATE VIBRATOR. NEXT SHOULD BE 6 TO 12 INCHES OF CRUSHED STONE (THE DEPTH IS DETERMINED BY THE CONDITION OF THE UNDERLYING SOIL, THE CLIMATE, AND THE ANTICIPATED TRAFFIC LOAD) THAT MUST ALSO BE COMPACTED. THE CRUSHED STONE IS COVERED BY 1 TO 1½ INCHES OF COURSE BEDDING SAND, INTO WHICH THE PAVERS ARE LAID, THEN PRESSED IN PLACE BY THE FLAT-PLATE VIBRATOR. ADDITIONAL SAND IS SWEPT BETWEEN THE PAVERS.

ONE FINAL ROUND OF COMPACTING COMPRESSES THE SAND EVENLY IN THE JOINTS, WHICH ALLOWS THE PAVERS TO SPREAD VERTICAL LOADS HORIZONTALLY, SO THE WEIGHT OF VEHICLES IS DIFFUSED. EDGE RESTRAINTS—TYPICALLY MADE OF PLASTIC, METAL, POURED CONCRETE, OR STONE—LINE THE SIDES OF THE DRIVE AND HOLD THE ENTIRE SYSTEM IN PLACE. “THE EDGE RESTRAINTS ARE CRUCIAL,” SAYS DONNA DENINNO, MARKETING DIRECTOR OF A NATIONAL PAVER-MAKERS ASSOCIATION. “THEY MAINTAIN THE PATTERN DESIGN AND PROPER JOINT SPACING, AND HELP ENSURE THE PAVERS WILL NOT CREEP APART.”

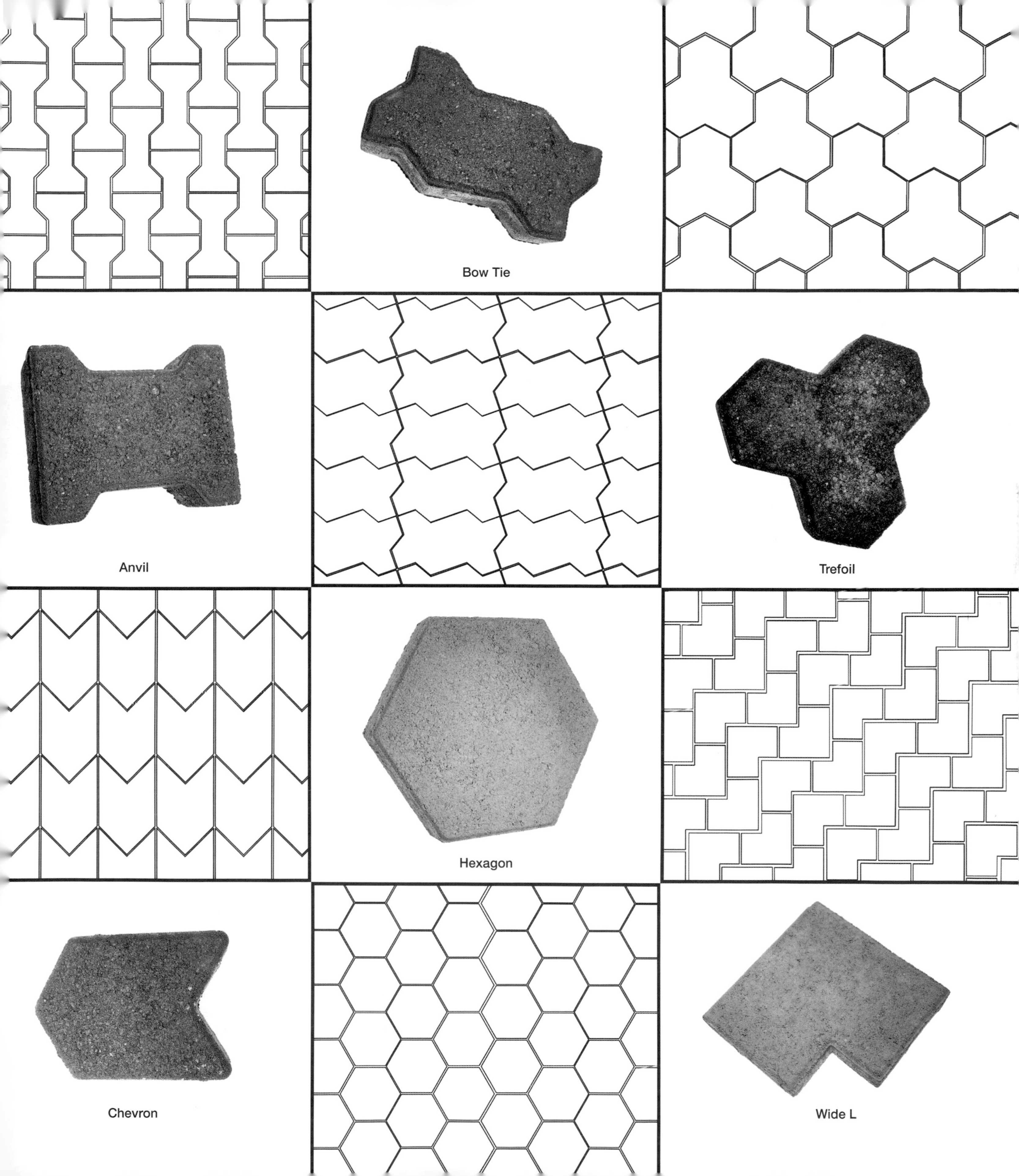

Bow Tie
Anvil
Trefoil
Hexagon
Chevron
Wide L

[building a patio]

they don't crack like poured concrete. Unlike asphalt, they don't have to be sealed and then resealed every couple of years. And if individual pavers do become cracked or broken, they can be removed and replaced without leaving ugly patches. Because of their strength, concrete pavers are entirely suitable for driveways as well as patios and walks.

Not surprisingly, the price tag for installed pavers is equally impressive, averaging two to three times the cost of asphalt and as much as twice the cost of poured concrete. But for many people, the aesthetic value alone justifies the extra cost. When laid out in a traditional herringbone or basket-weave pattern—or whatever design a home-owner imagines—pavers can create memorable results.

Poured concrete calls for careful attention to the details of mix, reinforcement, and finishing. The larger the area, the more important it is that professionals do the work. This holds true for driveways (below) as well as backyard patios.

SURFACES FOR PATIOS AND DRIVEWAYS

1. Plain concrete. **Provides a low-maintenance, level surface that is easy to clear of snow. Concrete will stain, and breaks down with exposure to road salt.**

2. Gravel. **Rounded surfaces are easier on tires and bare feet than jagged crushed stone. Requires a border to hold it in place and a fabric ground cover to keep weeds out.**

3. Stamped asphalt. **Wire templates pressed into fresh asphalt leave a textured surface that imitates brick. Can be deformed by excess heat and pressure.**

4. Colored asphalt. **Powdered pigment dissolved in an asphalt-based sealer provides color. Pigment must be reapplied every 2 to 5 years.**

5. Crushed stone. **Offers low cost and a rustic look. Type and color of stone varies with location. Driveway potholes form easily, and a gravel drive can be difficult to plow.**

6. Acid-stained concrete. **Stain penetrates the top 1/8 inch of concrete to impart color. Multiple colors may be combined to give the appearance of stone. Colors fade over time.**

7. Exposed aggregate. **A layer of concrete is washed from the surface to reveal the color and texture of the aggregate (gravel) beneath. The uneven surface is prone to freeze/thaw damage unless protected by acrylic sealers.**

8. Plain asphalt. **A mix of aggregate and asphalt laid over a gravel base. Must be sealed regularly with asphalt emulsion. Difficult to get a neat-looking surface.**

9. Pigmented concrete. **Colors (there are hundreds to choose from) are mixed into the concrete or dusted on while it is wet. The latter yields stronger hues, but chips reveal the gray beneath.**

10. Chip seal asphalt. **Gravel is rolled into a sticky top layer of asphalt emulsion. The surface has more texture and color than plain asphalt, but stones are apt to loosen.**

11. Cobblestone. **Belgian block (cut granite squares) or rounded river rock is expensive; the uneven surface makes snow-clearing difficult. Plants can grow between cobbles.**

12. Stamped concrete. **Patterns pressed into wet concrete leave texture that imitates other surfaces. The concrete is typically stained or pigmented as well.**

1
2
3
4
5
6
7
8
9
10
11
12

* * *

CREDITS

AUTHORS: Tom Baker, Alexandra Bandon, Joe Carter, Claudia Glenn Dowling, Ken Druse, Kathy Ehrich, Mark Feirer, Stephen Harrigan, Pamela Hartford, Jeanne Huber, Joseph Hurst-Wajszczuk, Peter Jensen, Hillary Johnson, Sebastian Junger, William A. Marsano, Jack McClintock, Michael McWilliams, George Nash, Sasha Nyary, Stephen L. Petranek, Hope Reeves, Curtis Rist, Mary Roach, Victoria C. Rowan, John Saladyga, Cynthia Sanz, William G. Scheller, Warren Schultz, Sara Stein, Richard Stepler, Jeff Taylor, Amy Virshup, Dennis Wedlick.

PHOTOGRAPHERS: William D. Adams, David Albanese, Christine Alicino, Peter Ardito, Art & Commerce Anthology, André Baranowski, David Bartolomi, Matthew Benson, John Blais, Peter Bosch, Christiana Ceppas, Jim Cooper, Ken Druse, Pete Eckert, Michael Grimm, Darrin Haddad, Mick Hales, Charles Harris, Forest History Society, Richard Howard, Grace Huang, Gary Hush, Andrew Kaufman, Keller & Keller, John Kernick, Kit Latham, Michael Mazzeo, Patricia McDonough, Joshua McHugh, Michael McLaughlin, Raymond Meeks, Gary Moss, J Michael Myers, Eric O'Connell, Benjamin Oliver, Rick Olivier, Ken Probst, Erik Rank, Paul Sanders, Scotts Co., Brian Smale, Brian Smith, Kolin Smith, Simon Watson, Alan Weintraub/Arcaid, Judy White, James Worrell, Joe Yutkins.

ILLUSTRATIONS: John Burgoyne, Tim Carroll, John Ferry, Bob Hambly, WGBH/Morash Assoc. Inc., Gregory Nemec, Mark Rosenshein, Douglas Tocco, Lester Walker, Manon Zinzell.

THIS OLD HOUSE® BOOKS
EDITOR: Mark Feirer
ART DIRECTOR: Jeanne Criscola
PRODUCTION COORDINATOR: Robert Hardin
COPY EDITOR: Tiffany Rhae Watson
YARD CARE CONSULTANT: Jeanne Huber

DIRECTOR, NEW PRODUCT DEVELOPMENT: Bob Fox

SPECIAL THANKS TO: Norm Abram, Steve Thomas, Tom Silva, Richard Trethewey, Bruce Irving and Russell Morash at the show; Roger Cook, landscape contractor for *This Old House* and *The Victory Garden*; Betsy Groban and Peter McGhee at WGBH; and Stephen VanHove and Anthony Wendling at Applied Graphics Technologies.

Funding for *This Old House* on public television is provided by State Farm Insurance Companies, Ace Hardware Corporation, The Minwax & Krylon Brands, and the Saturn Corporation.

« **In spring,** when lawns look their best, our optimism grows along with the burgeoning blades. »